CHALLENGES OF PRIMARY EDUCATION IN DEVELOPING COUNTRIES

To
My late father C. K. Unnikrishna Pillai
and my late sister Indira Menon

Challenges of Primary Education in Developing Countries

Insights from Kenya

PAUL P. W. ACHOLA
Department of Sociology
Kenyatta University, Nairobi

VIJAYAN K. PILLAI
School of Social Work
University of Texas at Arlington, Texas

Ashgate

Aldershot • Burlington USA • Singapore • Sydney

Published by
Ashgate Publishing Limited
Gower House
Croft Road
Aldershot
Hampshire GU11 3HR
England

Ashgate Publishing Company
131 Main Street
Burlington, VT 05401-5600 USA

Ashgate website: http://www.ashgate.com

British Library Cataloguing in Publication Data
Achola, Paul P. W.
  Challenges of primary education in developing countries :
  insights from Kenya
  1.Education, Elementary - Kenya 2.Dropouts - Kenya
  3.Dropouts - Kenya - Prevention
  I.Title II.Pillai, Vijayan K.
  372.9'6762

Library of Congress Control Number: 00-107885

ISBN 1 84014 889 6

Printed in Great Britain by
Antony Rowe Ltd, Chippenham, Wiltshire.

Contents

List of Tables and Figure

Preface

This book is an attempt at describing the components of primary school wastage in Kenya. Research on wastage in developing countries suffers from a number of drawbacks. First, very few studies have probed into the concept of wastage. As a result, the interlocking relationships among the various indicators of wastage were never fully developed. Secondly, most studies in the past have focused on one of the dimensions of primary school wastage, dropout. Among the two remaining components of wastage, the first, non-enrolment, has been often dealt with at the macro level given the availability of national census data. The second component, repetition, has more or less remained under investigated. Finally, the need for micro level studies for investigating wastage has been well argued in the education literature. However, quantitative approaches at the micro level have often ignored the importance of perceptions of the wastage problem among educational personnel. This book is an attempt at addressing the above mentioned drawbacks. The methodological approach is evaluative. The socio-economic context of wastage in Kenya is that of an agricultural economy, characterized by a low level of economic development. To the extent that developing countries share the characteristics of the Kenyan economy, this study provides useful findings for formulating policies to eradicate wastage in primary education in developing countries.

Acknowledgments

Several chapters of this book were written while the first author was a Fulbright Research Scholar at the University of North Texas. We thank the Fulbright Foundation, Department of Sociology at the University of North Texas, and the School of Social Work at the University of Texas at Arlington for providing us the logistical support necessary for completing this manuscript. The first author would like to express his profound gratitude to the Vice Chancellor and the administration at the Kenyatta University for extending their unconditional support during the initial phase of this study. We would like to extend our sincere thanks to Dr. T.S. Sunil, University of North Texas, and Mr. Vivian Correa, University of Texas at Arlington for their competent assistance throughout the course of this project.

1   Introduction

Perhaps one of the most pressing social and political problems facing the educational system in the developing world today is a high attrition rate among primary school goers. The terms wastage has been used to label a number of broadly related problems associated with high attrition or dropout rates. Why, it may be asked, should anyone bother about failure by some citizens of a country (which wastage implies) to receive full primary education or its equivalent? Does attending primary school or failure to do so make any difference in the lives of those involved and in the communities in which they belong? Should one not focus research on higher education, such as secondary and university levels, which ostensibly better prepare their recipients for skills training or direct participation in both the labor market and community life? Penetrating as these questions may be, they are to an extent based on a wrong premise, namely an ideological view that places a strong premium on the economic benefits of schooling.

The singular obsession with education as an economic concept has led to disastrous consequences ranging from frustrations and disillusionment by the 'educated unemployed' and their sponsors (usually parents) with the costs of schooling. Lack of immediate economic gain from schooling has also lead to the devaluation of schooling by a skeptical public including school-age youth in many new states. A recasting of perspectives on the place of schooling, particularly the primary school cycle, is desirable and urgent. The position taken here is not to deny the economic benefits that schooling only confers on individuals, but rather to map these within the context of broader 'benefits to schooling'. In our view, the need for a study on primary school education is all the more pressing when the content of discourse is 'wastage' in primary education.

The Centrality of Primary Schooling

One may take as a point of departure the fact that in the contemporary world many communities rely on schooling as the major provider of education.

1

There are, of course, communities which do not actively engage in schooling and as a result depend largely on the family to promote education among their members. It is a fact, however, that such communities are few, isolated and endangered; they are not important social actors in the communal life of their nation states.

As a matter of fact, the United Nations isolated education as a key factor in the new social order that emerged after World War II and made efforts to correct the marginalization of groups on account of lack of access to basic education. In 1948 nation states through the General Assembly of the newly established United Nations, authored the document now widely known as the Universal Declaration of Human Rights. Article 26 of this document is directly relevant to the discussion here since it states that participation in schooling is a fundamental right:

> Everyone has the right to education. Education shall be free at least in the elementary and fundamental stages. Elementary education shall be compulsory. Technical and professional education shall be made generally available and higher education shall be equally accessible to all on the basis of merit.

At first it was not clear why the authors of the Universal Declaration of Human Rights regarded education (read schooling) to be so important that everyone should receive it. A little over a decade later, plenty of insight on this issue was provided by a complementary Declaration of the Rights of the Child proclaimed by the same General Assembly of the United Nations in 1959. In reference to education, Principle 7 of the Declaration on the Rights of the Child urged that:

> The child is entitled to receive education, which shall be free and compulsory, at least in the elementary stages. He/she shall be given an education which will promote his/her general culture and enable him/her, on a basis of equal opportunity, to develop his/her abilities, individual judgment, and sense of moral and social responsibility, and to become a useful member of society. The best interests of the child shall be the guiding principle of those responsible for his/her education and guidance.

As is apparent from the Declaration of the Rights of the Child, not only did 'free' nations of the world following World War II re-emphasize the imperatives of education at the elementary or fundamental stage, but also provided a rationale, however vague. Education was regarded as necessary because it molds the learners into rational thinkers and promotes change agents within their social milieu.   Given these perceived benefits, communities were expected to regard education at the basic, elementary level as a public good for which they were to be fully responsible. The pledge was to make such education free and compulsory. But whether or not those who manage the education enterprise are often guided by the best interests of the child is a contentious issue.

What case do we ourselves make for emphasis on widening access to primary school education? Three broad arguments are particularly relevant in this regard. First, primary education is a foundation for later learning, whether that learning is formal or informal. The type of curricula and pedagogic approaches learners are exposed to at the foundation primary school level does influence their capacities for later learning. In addition, they also influence the intensity of intellectual curiosity, reading habits and dexterity with calculation tasks. Stated in summary form, experience with schooling during the foundation years at the primary level can enhance an individual's capacity for learning.

The second factor in favor of focus on primary school education is its linkage to literacy. Literacy, defined as the ability of an individual to at least read and write simple sentences in any one language, is better promoted for large sections of a citizenry through attendance of primary school education. A major emphasis of the primary school curriculum in virtually all countries of the world is to impart the skills of reading and writing. The importance of literacy is rooted in research findings, which show that primary schooling does instill information rendering pupils well informed. Furthermore, it reduces xenophobia, improves self-confidence, enhances productivity and promotes health seeking behavior thus increasing life expectancy for both the individual and dependents. The fact that the provision of primary school education and literacy go hand in hand is now widely recognized.

It can be easily argued that easy access to primary education is a wiser and less costly option in the long-term. Alternative literacy promotion programs tend on the whole to be expensive. These include literacy training for adults, functional literacy (literacy incorporated within a development project), and literacy campaigns. The unit cost of effective alternative literacy programs is generally higher than that associated with primary schooling and the outcomes tend to be more short-lived. All this leads to the conclusion that a more prudent national education policy is that which encourages widespread participation in primary schooling in the hope that corrective measures which need to be undertaken to foster literacy for those who missed out on schooling will be few and inexpensive. Nonetheless, we recognize that in the short-term many countries, especially the new states must continue to rely on these costly alternatives in their efforts to promote literacy.

The final point we make in support of primary schooling is evidence regarding rates of return to different levels of education. There is consistent and ample evidence that purely in economic terms, investment in primary education yields higher rates of return, both private and social, than investment in secondary and tertiary education. Because the measurement of rates of return include parameters which are essentially monetary, the fact that one level of education may have a higher rate of return than another level should not be taken to mean an underlying superiority in terms of benefits. Unfortunately, many economists of education have used evidence about the higher rates of return to primary schooling to advocate for the transfer of resources from secondary and tertiary education to the primary level for new states. It is not our intention to detail the various aspects of this debate, but our position is that an increase in the number of the graduates of secondary and, especially, tertiary education can contribute toward a critical mass necessary for technological adaptation and innovation. It is on these graduates that the new states must rely for technological survival and national leadership and not the graduates of primary education whose cognitive and leadership skills are at best rudimentary. In this sense, concerted efforts must be made by the new states to promote all levels of education if dependence on foreign, mainly American and European, technical personnel is to be considerably scaled down in the medium and long-term.

In view of our perspective as stated above, our concern with wastage should be seen as an attempt to focus on a level that is the 'substructure' of education in any contemporary society. The quality of the curriculum and student experiences at this basic level have a strong bearing on learning outcomes at the secondary and tertiary levels. In this respect, it is relevant to provide an account of the aims of primary education as well as its duration in Kenya as these tend to influence student's access, retention and success at this level of the schooling process (Eshiwani, 1984; Eshiwani et al., 1988). Although particular reference is made to Kenya, many of the issues covered in this book apply quite well to many other African countries.

Evolution of Primary Education in the Kenyan Setting

Apart from Islamic koranic schools at the Kenyan coast, which accompanied the arrival of Arab traders in the 14th century, formal education in Kenya was established more elaborately by Christian missionaries at the start of the 20th century. The work of establishing mission schools started at the coast in 1846 when two German missionaries, Johann Krapf and Johann Rabman opened a school at Rabbi near Mombassa. It was, however, the completion of the Kenya-Uganda railway in the early 1900s that gave impetus to the opening up of more schools. The railway line from Mombassa on the Indian Ocean coast and Port Florence (now Kisume) on Lake Victoria in West Kenya was completed in 1901 and the line to Kampala from Nakuru a few years later.

The building of the railway which opened up Kenya's hinterland and the Anglo-German agreement of 1890, gave rise to three factors that influenced the development of education from the very beginning. First, it made the Kenyan inlands accessible to a large settler white community. Second, the large Indian labor force that assisted in the construction of the railway was encouraged by the British colonial government to settle in the country. Third, many Africans whose land had been alienated and others mainly through the use of coercive labor laws and practices, were uprooted from their normal settings and appended to the colonial white settler economy.

In effect, three distinct racial communities were compelled by the modus operandi of the colonial economy to interact with one another. This scenario gave rise to a 'racial question' spearheaded by the hegemonic European settler community. Around 1907, organized interests on behalf of this community used the newly established Legislative Council to commit the government to a policy of separate development for the three races namely Europeans, Asians and Africans. In the education sphere, this policy was succinctly formulated in Professor Frazier's report of 1909 which endorsed the principle of different systems of education for the three racial groups with Africans earmarked to receive technical education (Hughes, 1979). The missionaries were encouraged to implement this policy through a program of grants in aid for 'industrial' education, the level of the grant being pegged to the level of effort (more easily measured in terms of enrolment).

A turning point in the provision of education under colonialism in Kenya came in 1911 with the establishment of a Department of Education. The launching of this department marked the start of more extensive government-missionary cooperation in education on the one hand and the government's direct initiatives in the provision of education on the other hand. Mission schools obtained increased subsidies for education from the government so that about sixty or so mission schools in operation around 1912 were able over the next few years to increase their enrolment of African pupils (Soja, 1968; Thias and Carnoy, 1972). Meanwhile the Department of Education started to open up schools of its own in earnest. Schools for European and Indian children were opened up in all the major towns and areas of settlement namely Nairobi, Mombassa, Kisumi, Eldoret and Nakuru. The Arabs also had schools opened for their children in Mombassa in 1912 and in Malindi in 1919 (Thias and Carnoy, 1972). These early direct government provision of schools bypassed African children.

The years following the end of World War I were characterized by agitation from African leaders for better educational opportunities for African children. Agitations led by Kenyan African World War I veterans succeeded in opening the doors of opportunity for education to African children. This education facilitated the acquisition of white-collar jobs. As a result of these experiences and perceptions, Africans called for greater expansion in enrolment at the primary school level and opening up of the secondary school level for African children.

The colonial government responded by setting up an Education Commission in 1919 with the mandate to look into the unsatisfactory status of education for all races in the protectorate. The commission made a vague recommendation to the effect that while the provision of education would remain a major responsibility of the missionaries, the government should increase its role in the provision of education. The Education Commission of the Phelps-Stokes Fund of 1924 addressed African concerns about education more directly by calling for quantitative expansion and qualitative improvement of African education in the colony. One objective of this qualitative improvement was to give Africans academic type of education similar to that available to Euro and Asian children.

The government's reaction was again characteristically gradualist and piecemeal. It stuck to its philosophy and policy of separate education curricula for the three races but sought to placate African concerns by establishing in 1925, a permanent Advisory Committee on Education with a network of area school committees on which Local Native Councils (LNCs), the main administrative organs for Africans, were represented. These LNCs collected funds from Africans to be spent on establishing schools outside missionary control. The following year (1926) the government's response to the call for an academic curriculum for African children took the form of examination and certification for African pupils who had completed primary schooling. The government also established the Alliance High School and added three others before the outbreak of World War II in 1939 as a partial measure to meet African demands for secondary education (Thias and Carnoy, 1972).

It is significant to note that each of the four secondary schools established during this interim period was to largely serve one of the four major African ethnic groups namely Kikenyu, Luc, Luhya and Kamba. The regional and ethnic basis of education that had been laid by the participation of LNCs in the provision of primary school education was now extended to the secondary level; the legacy of this ethnic nature of educational opportunities was subsequently to be a lingering feature of Kenyan education.

Although reliable enrolment data are not available it appears that the enrolment of girls in both primary and secondary schools lagged far below that of boys from the very beginning. This partly was a logical consequence of colonial political ideology, which was both statist and patriarchal. It is for example instructive that out of some 300 pupils enrolled in government sponsored secondary schools in 1945; only 2 (two) were girls (Thias and Carnoy, 1972).

The onset of World War II, the war itself and the years immediately following the end of the war, marked a turning point in the development of education in Kenya and in colonial Africa generally. The war exposed African servicemen who had participated in it to other cultures and new technologies. Soon after the war, India, in 1947 and Pakistan in 1948 became independent states from British rule. These two events reinforced the demand for independence in European colonies in Africa. Soon it became apparent that colonies had to be prepared for self-government. These pressures dovetailed into the beginning of 'mass education' at the primary school level in Kenya. Since this book focuses primarily on issues of universalized access to basic (primary) education, key timings of benchmark events in the evolution of mass education in Kenya need highlighting if we are to provide an effective description of the subject. These benchmarks include government commissioned development plans and multi-state international conferences often sponsored by one or more of the United Nations agencies.

Benchmarks in the Move Towards Mass Education in Kenya 1963-1970

So far, the evidence we have presented is one of great reluctance on the part of colonial authorities to widen educational opportunities, at all levels, for children of African Kenyan decent.   Nonetheless, more opportunities gradually become available as a result of pressure on the colonial agents from African leaders before independence in 1963, and from African masses and international pressure groups on African leaders after independence.

Persistent action in favor of greater opportunities in (primary) education by African leaders following the end of World War II culminated in the 1948 Ten Year Plan for Education in which the colonial functionaries aimed to provide 50% of school-going age children with education lasting six years. The Ten Year Plan for Education found further official sanction in the Beecher Education Commission of 1949, which went beyond the Ten Year Plan in making the following three recommendations (Stabler, 1969).

> a) That primary school educational facilities are provided in areas of Kenya in which such facilities were lacking;
> b) That attention is paid not only to quantitative expansion of primary education, but to its qualitative improvement as well;
> c) That in view of some negative aspects of the industrial-and agricultural-oriented curriculum for African children, these be improved and that about 5% of the African pupils who completed primary school continue with secondary education.

Presumably in order to improve the quality of the graduates, the duration of the primary school cycle for African pupils was altered in 1952. Before this date, the system consisted of six years of primary schooling (standards/grades 1 to 6), two years of junior secondary (Forms I and II), and four years of senior secondary (Forms 3 to 6).   This was altered in 1952 to three levels, namely, four years of primary school (standards/grades 1 to 4), four years of intermediate school (standards/grades 5 to 8) and four years of secondary school (Forms 1 to 4 or grades 9 to 12).   The first eight years, consisting of primary and intermediate phases, constituted the full primary school cycle; and although the secondary school component had four years, students had the option to leave after appearing for the Kenya African Secondary Examination (KASE) given at the end of the second year in Form 2. The new structuring of the school cycle did not alter its 12 year duration. Furthermore, the implementation of the new educational program remained the responsibility of LNCs which used District Education Boards (DEBs) as the administrative vehicle for the management of primary schools. Since ANCs differed markedly in their resource base, their use in the management and financing of education resulted in glaring inequalities in the provision of and access to education. Thus, although the educational reforms of 1952 led to increase in enrolment at the primary school level, there were considerable regional inequalities in enrolments.

At the same time, the rapid expansion of primary education for African pupils both before and after the Beecher Commission resulted in a fall in standards partly because of many poorly educated and trained teachers who run the system. Inspection of these teachers was equally inadequate as were learning facilities and materials. As a result performance in key examinations, such as those for matriculation into upper primary and into secondary schools, was usually quite poor.

Primary education had been made compulsory for both European and Asian children of appropriate age about a decade earlier in 1943. Children of these two groups were therefore spared the vagaries of educational participation experienced by African children.

The outbreak of the Mau Mau Revolt in 1952 did slow down enrolment in primary education as it led to the closing of independent schools and to disruption of schooling in Central Kenya among the Kenyan ethnic communities perceived by colonial authorities as allied to them. But as soon as the Mau Mau revolt was contained in 1956, the demands for more primary and secondary school opportunities for Africans increased considerably. This was in large part due to the realization that with Ghana's independence from Britain in 1957, Kenya, and other British territories in Africa would soon be self-governing. In the eleven years between 1948 and 1959, total primary school enrolment figures for pupils of African descent had nearly tripled from 261,735 to just over 712,900)(Thias and Conroy, 1972).

The second benchmark in the expansion of primary educational opportunities for African children in Kenya was the Conference of African States on the Development of Education in Africa held in Addis Ababa, Ethiopia in May 1961 under the aegis of UNESCO and the United Nation's Economic Commission for Africa. Although Kenya was as yet not politically independent, it was among the thirty nine African countries participating in the conferences. One key resolution adopted at this conference was the need to develop primary and adult education with a view to attaining universal literacy by 1980. The Kenya African National Union (KANU), the political party expected to form the first post-colonial government, reaffirmed the goal of Universal primary education in its manifesto of 1962.

Enrolment in education, particularly at the primary school level, rose rapidly as the date of political independence approached. For example at the launching of the Ten Year Plan for Education in 1948 some 261,735 pupils of African Kenyan descent were enrolled in primary education. This figure about trebled to about 719,500 by 1959, an increase of nearly 180%. On the eve of independence in 1962, the number of African pupils in Kenyan primary schools had reached 935,766 representing an increase of 357% over the 1948 figures.

The enrolment figures available for this period just before independence in 1963 and the few years following it show that attention from school and repetition of grades was already evident. For example, over 30% of the 1959 grade 1 cohort had already left prematurely by grade 5 and about 33% by the final year of primary school in grade 7 in 1965. For this 1959 grade one cohort, repetition was very small and occurred only in grades 3 and 4. Both the steep decline in members by grade 5 and the modest repetitions in grades 3 and 4 existed because of a screening examination called the Competitive Entrance Examination (CEE) taken at the end of the fourth grade.

The 1962 cohort that started grade 1 on the eve of independence and was considerably larger than the 1959 cohort, and it displayed trends typical of similar cohorts after independence. This 1962 grade 1 cohort did not experience the Competitive Entrance Examination as this was removed with independence in 1963. Notwithstanding, only 71 per cent of them reached grade 5. Yet as much as about 80% and 86% reached grades 6 and 7, respectively. In other words, with the removal of CEE in grade 4, repetition now shifted to grades 6 and 7 in the hope that this practice would facilitate better performance in the Kenya Preliminary Examination (KPE) given at the end of grade 7.

But let us turn to broader issues. After independence in 1963, Kenya found itself critically deficient in secondary school and tertiary education graduates. This situation was to be expected since colonial authorities had for years limited the access of African children to these levels of schooling. A few years before independence two important studies had highlighted the need to expand secondary and tertiary education levels. In 1961, the Kenyan colonial government and the British government engaged the services of the World Bank in a survey of economic development in Kenya. In the education sector, the Bank identified the bottleneck at the secondary level as an issue for urgent attention. The bank did not overlook the need to expand the primary school sector and therefore recommended that local school district boards fund expansion at this level. The second study on Kenyan education was that of V. L. Griffith. Griffiths recommended urgent expansion of the secondary education level to provide the country with trained manpower that would be required on attainment of independence. Griffith's study found popular demand for universal primary education but did not recommend its implementation largely to avoid the prospect of competition for resources between this sector and secondary education.

Given the thrust of education policy statements just before independence, it came as no surprise the first education commission appointed by the new independent government, the Dmide Commission of 1964 supported the objective of priority expansion of secondary education. The commission cautioned that the immediate implementation of universal primary education was not financially viable but nonetheless endorsed its implementation in the long run. In conformity to this recommendation in the First National Development Plan of 1964-70, the new government specified that emphasis during the Plan period would be on the expansion of higher levels of education and gearing up for the human resource needs of the modern sector while making provisions of facilities for a slow but steady increase in primary school enrolment.

In consequence, during the period covered by the First National Development Plan, primary school enrolment grew at a slower rate than secondary school enrolment. Nonetheless, the increase in primary school enrolment for Kenya would have been much higher if two main barriers had been removed. These barriers were wide regional variations in enrolment and the charging of school fees which discouraged the children of the poor from enrolling in school. In this respect the 75 percent participation rate for boys and the 50 percent participation rate for girls given for this period mask wide regional and group variations.

Primary Education Between 1970 and 1995

A diverse but interrelated number of external forces and rather impromptu internal pressures influenced the growth of primary school education in the two and a half decades between 1970 and 1995. The major external agencies focusing on education in this period were UNICEF, UNESCO and the World Bank. At the same time, Kenya had by now put in place a number of policy documents which also assisted in shaping its educational priorities and programs. Below we discuss the interplay of these external and internal forces that have shaped the development of Kenyan primary education since 1970.

To begin with, although the International Labor Organization (ILO) had sent an evaluation mission to Kenya in 1972 which recommended in part that the government embark on basic education and make the proposed nine year basic education course heavily vocational. These recommendations were not immediately implemented. The government was at that time busy supporting community initiatives to improve prospects of employment for secondary school graduates through the establishment of technical training institutions called Harambee (self-help) Institutes of Technology. Then starting in early 1974 and through to 1975, several international studies emphasized that Third World countries need to refocus their educational systems on basic education.

A group of Western donor agencies operating under the Bellagio Consortium commissioned a study, which rationalized the need for them to put emphasis on funding basic education initiatives. In like manner, both UNICEF and the World Bank engaged the services of the International Council for Educational Development (ICED) to review their educational policies towards the Third World. The Bellagio Consortium recommendations resulted in meetings of English- and French-speaking African educators held in Nairobi, Kenya in August and October, 1974 by UNICEF and UNESCO. These meetings revealed and confirmed the donors' common goal in favor of basic education but left each country free to determine what it considered as basic education. Two documents emerged from the ICED study for the World Bank. The Education Sector Working Paper issued in December 1974 and Rural Development Sector Policy Paper published in February 1975.

Regarding education, the two World Bank documents stressed strikingly similar goals which included: a) the development of functionally relevant skills, integrated with overall rural development strategies; b) mass participation in education and the development through integrated use of expanded primary schooling and complementary non-formal education programs; c) greater equity through equalizing educational opportunities and linking these to broader social policies; d) increasing efficiency by defining objectives more specifically and making qualitative improvements to reduce wastage; and e) improving management and planning including changes in the organization and finance of educational systems. The World Bank policy was, therefore, decidedly in favor of basic education, with primary schooling targeted as the major means of promoting it, and the targeting of various groups to enhance more equitable access to schooling. This new focus laid to rest the Bank's educational policy of the 1960-1970 decade of priority for secondary and higher education and technical training. This shift tallied with the policies of donor agencies about required reforms in primary education in new states and the priority of basic education therein.

These shifting postures by the international agencies appear to have evoked three distinct responses from the Kenya government. First on the occasion of the country's tenth independence celebrations in December 1973, a presidential decree stipulated that starting in January 1974, charging school fees was to cease for lower primary school grades (standards 1 to 4). The implementation of this presidential directive had an immediate effect on primary school enrolment within these lower grades; the number of students rose from 1.8 million the previous year to about 2.8 million, an increase of some 1 million pupils, in January 1974.

The second response was the appointment of a National Committee on Education   Objectives and Policies (NCEOP) in 1975, to examine within the Kenyan contest the concerns about education raised by donor agencies, the ILO Mission of 1972 and the various World Bank documents.   The committee's report accepted the ILO recommendations on basic education and the lengthening of primary education to a nine year basic cycle, the improvement of facilities, greater vocationalization of the school curriculum and a revamping of the examination system.

In January 1979, the government's third response to pressures to expand access to primary schooling, was the removal of school fees in the upper primary school grades 5 to 7. This unknotting of the fees barrier resulted in an immediate upsurge in primary school enrolments that year just as had happened in 1974. This abolition of school fees in 1974 and 1979 was a necessary but by no means a sufficient condition for equitable participation in primary schooling in Kenya.

If the Kenya Government found it easy to remove school fees from primary school education, the implementation of far-reaching educational reforms proved more intractable. Thus, the comprehensive reforms advocated by various international agencies and which had been endorsed by the National Committee on Educational Objectives and Policies in 1975remained unimplemented until 1979. After the General Elections of 1979, a new Ministry of Basic Education was launched to steer the implementation of the NCEOP proposals. But the pervasive lack of political will, especially among policy makers and civil service bureaucrats, to implement the serious educational reforms that had been advocated became apparent. School committees that were expected to mobilize communities for raising funds to construct new classrooms required for the proposed basic education, worked with little enthusiasm and were therefore ineffective.

This general reluctance to implement meaningful educational reforms, and other pressing factors such as mounting school leaver unemployment and increasing marginalization of groups historically excluded from mainstream education in Kenya, undergirded a presidential announcement in 1982. The presidential announcement directed that starting in 1985 the country was to implement a new education system consisting of eight years of primary education, four years of secondary education and a minimum of four years of university education (the 8-4-4 system). The announcement stressed that the curriculum of the new education system was to have a strong vocational bias in order to enhance prospects of gainful employment for primary and secondary school leavers who would be unable to continue with higher schooling. True to the announcement, the 8-4-4 system of education was launched in January 1985 with many attendant problems. Major among these were insufficient learning resources especially those needed to handle the teaching and practice of technical-cum-practical subjects, inadequate classrooms in some areas and widespread lack of trained and retrained personnel to handle many aspects of the new curriculum.

Some four years after Kenya embraced the 8-4-4 system of education, four international agencies that had been working behind the scenes regarding the eradication of illiteracy, teamed up to sponsor a 'World Conference on Education for All: Meeting Basic Learning Needs'. The four international agencies namely UNESCO, UNICEF, UNDP and the World Bank announced at the beginning of 1989 that the World Conference on Education for All was to be held near Bangkok, Thailand in March of 1990. These four agencies in particular urged and obtained the participation of many smaller agencies both private and public in support of country efforts to plan for the implementation of the main World Conference goals. Kenya was among those countries that participated in preparations for and the deliberations of the World Conference on Education for All held in Jomtien, Thailand between March 5th and 9th, 1990. Similarly, in September of the same year, Kenya participated in the deliberations of the World Summit for children in New York City.

In identifying with both the World Conference on Education for All and the World Summit on the Rights of the Child, and signing their Declarations, Kenya committed itself to the educational goals of the two world conferences. In effect, Kenya pledged to ensure: completion of primary education by at least 80% of the primary school age children (14 year olds) by the year 2000: universal access to basic education by the year 2000; and reduction in adult illiteracy to at least one half of its 1990 level (which for Kenya was about 30% for men and 59% for women) by the year 2000.

A National Task Force was established in Kenya to canvass for and monitor the implementation of the stated goals. In 1992, this task force, operating under the aegis of the Kenya National Commission for UNESCO, Ministry of Education, published a document on National Strategies for the Implementation of Education for All. The Task Force also obtained official government approval of this document.

In addition, UNICEF and UNESCO have organized several regional meetings in Africa to assess national performance records in pursuit of the Jomtien Education for All objectives. Kenya remained committed to education for all. In general, more success has been registered in the promotion of non-formal education programs mainly with support from non-governmental organizations. The primary school sector objectives and those about the reduction of adult illiteracy are unlikely to be met in the stated time frame due largely to lingering social and economic constraints and nascent political unrest. The primary school sector in particular has since 1987 experienced an upward spiral in wastage while adult literacy programs have increasingly experienced higher rates of non-enrolment.

2   Research on Wastage in Kenya

In this chapter the operational meaning of the concept of wastage in education is presented.   A conceptual framework for explaining and therefore understanding, the processes of educational wastage is formulated.   The chapter concludes with a review of literature on educational wastage in the Kenyan context.   As much as possible in the review of the literature on educational wastage, the formulated conceptual framework is used as an organizing frame.   It is important to state at the outset that the utility of the conceptual framework is in our view, its ability to clarify those factors linked to wastage in education and not its comprehensiveness as a model for accounting for educational wastage.   Indeed, we make no claim at all about the comprehensiveness of the conceptual framework.

The Meaning of Educational Wastage

There is a strong tendency in academic writing to define educational wastage primarily from the disciplinary perspective of economics.   The thrust is mainly to quantify the cost of educational wastage in resource investment terms. The opportunity cost of wastage for a school system or an educational system is ultimately what has to be documented in proximate monetary units.   Typically then, this perspective views wastage in education as: the total number of pupil-years spent by repeaters and dropouts. Total wastage is measured as the proportion of the total number of pupil-years spent by repeaters and dropouts to the total number of pupils years accruing to a student cohort of which the repeaters and dropouts are an integral part (UNESCO, 1984; Loxley, 1987).

The economic definition of educational wastage given above can be more clearly expressed as the proportion of the number of pupil-years for repeaters and dropouts of cohort 1 to the total number of pupils for cohort 1.

This expresses the degree of efficiency of the school or educational system to process students through it in the minimum years stipulated to complete the particular educational cycle.

The two components of wastage mentioned above namely repeaters and dropouts require definition. Repeaters are those pupils who in a given school year remain in the same grade (class or standard as the case may be) in which they were the previous school year. They more or less go over the same material they were exposed to the previous year. In other words, they undergo a process of repetition of the grade as well as the curriculum material assigned for coverage in the particular grade. Each school year repeated is regarded as wastage from two points of view. First, it means occupying a slot that should have gone to a more deserving (i.e. non-repeating) student given that class sizes have an upper limit. Second, a repeating student uses more of the school resources than should be the case if repetition did not occur. An example may suffice here. Suppose a particular pupil J has repeated grades one, three and five in a seven year primary education cycle. Such a pupil has spent ten pupil years instead of seven. The wastage occurs in terms of the displacement of three pupils whose slots were filled by the repeater, and the cumulative per pupil cost associated with the three extra school years taken up by the repeater.

We next need to describe dropouts. Dropouts are pupils whose attendance of school ceases before they complete the final year of the educational cycle in which they are enrolled. In other words, they exit from the educational cycle prematurely. From the economically inclined definition of wastage presented in the foregoing paragraphs, a student (or pupil) who drops out early in the educational cycle without repeating, contributes relatively slightly to wastage compared to a student who drops out after several repetitions or who drops out with nearly most of the grades in the cycle completed (say grade six in a seven year educational cycle).

Scholars who define and undertake research on educational wastage in terms of school specific processes of repetition and dropout concur that most school systems have in place mechanisms for screening children. Some children are allowed to matriculate through the educational cycle uninterrupted; others go through after experiencing lags or delays; and some are compelled by circumstances to leave without completing the cycle. Although these scholars agree about screening in schools, they coalesce into two contending camps regarding criteria used in screening pupils (Levy, 1971; UNESCO, 1980; Chan, 1984; Ekstrom, Avertz, Pollack and Rock, 1986; Grissom and Shepard, 1989; Kelly, 1995).

The first group of scholars, heavily influenced by a functionalist theoretical perspective, refer to premature departure from school as dropping out. Their analytical framework is essentially one of establishing the correlates of exit from school, which within the school system are perceived to include student's social networks, attitudes, scholastic performance and family social milieu. Termination of schooling is viewed largely as failure by the individual student to cope with school norms, practices and expectations.

The second cluster of scholars, influenced largely by a Marxian or radical theory, attributes termination of schooling to structural inequalities inherent in a society. These inequalities are embedded in the economic, political and social structures of society and manifest themselves in differential schooling outcomes. Children from disadvantaged groups and family backgrounds in terms of these attributes tend to be screened out of meaningful schooling process. Thus, the children who leave school are push outs since they are eliminated by circumstances over which they have little or no control. To say that children dropout of school is to blame the victim (Bowles and Aintis, 1976; Verhine and Pita de Melo, 1988).

The disagreement in the perspectives of the two groups of scholars just mentioned is reconcilable. The difference between them is one of emphasis rather than of omission. We need to draw attention to the partial way in which educational wastage has thus far been defined and explained.

In the first place, even if we accept that wastage in education stems primarily from repetition and dropout, the consequences are broader than lost monetary investment and the opportunity cost in the form of botched potential enrollees. Wastage has also to include potential or actual illiteracy on the part of those who only partially attend, or totally miss out on, primary education. The illiterates forego meaningful development of their intellectual and, at times, complex practical skills. Their capacity to widen their intellectual perspectives and world view are under-cut by an incapacity to read, write and to manipulate numbers. In contemporary context, such persons run the risk of being left out of the vast array of information technology and information necessary to achieve social and economic mobility.

In the second place, to define educational wastage solely in terms of grade repetition (or grade retention) and dropout (or push-out), is to pay attention only to the supply side of education while overlooking or even ignoring the demand side. Both processes refer to children who have been supplied to the educational system. Left out of consideration are children who do not get access to schooling at all. The school system seems unaware of their existence or the educational system regards them with benign silence if not neglect. These children may fall into four broad categories: those who have only a vague idea about schooling; those who know about schooling but do not want anything to do with it and are supported in this by their parents and communities; those whose parents desire schooling but who themselves resist schooling; and those who along with their parents want schooling but have no access either because there are no schools or they cannot afford the costs of schooling.

In other words, these children remain outside the school system and constitute part of the primary school-age population that is not enrolled. This experience of non-enrolment is another important dimension of educational wastage. They are, from the context of the political system, worse off than repeaters and late dropouts because they have missed out on laying a foundation for literacy and meaningful participation in contemporary society where the written word is a vital key to effective participation in one's community. This lack of effective participation is a loss to the wider polity.

In this study then, educational wastage is conceptualized to include three components namely non-enrolment, repetition and dropout. Non-enrolment as has been implied, means failure on the part of those children of school-going age to enroll in school for whatever reason. It fundamentally represents the failure of the school system to attract all children to school whether enlisting in school is compulsory or voluntary. It is our position, therefore, that the educational system of any country should not be made to look better than it is by avoiding to be responsible for the extent of non-enrolment as part of its wastage problem.

Both repetition and dropout will be used in this study in the sense in which they have been defined and explained in the earlier paragraphs. We attach no moral valuation on these two terms. In this sense, we have no quarrel with the use of such competing nomenclature as grade retention or grade flunking; similarly, the equivalent use of push-out or fade-out in place of dropout (Kelly,1995).

Research on educational wastage has attempted to explore the causes of this phenomenon and its various components, the correlates thereof, the consequences of repetition and dropping out and policy options for their amelioration. There has been a strong tendency to explain such components of educational wastage as repetition and dropout in terms of the characteristics or qualities of repeaters and dropouts (Mann, 1986). A well considered conceptual framework to assist in organizing studies on educational wastage and in understanding its underlying correlates is generally lacking not withstanding the existence of massive literature to make a formulation possible. Effort made so far at developing conceptual frameworks for understanding educational wastage has been narrow in focus thus yielding only partial explanations (Natricello et al., 1986; Finn, 1989). There is a need, therefore to develop a more elaborate conceptual framework that can enhance our understanding of the correlates of the various components of educational wastage, which have been identified in this study as non-enrolment, repetition and dropout.

Toward a Conceptual Framework of Educational Wastage

Any useful conceptual framework for understanding the major correlates of wastage in education should include its key components of non-enrolment, repetition and dropout. A careful synthesis of the theoretical as well as empirically based literature on wastage in education should suggest the relationship among the three different components of educational wastage as shown schematically in Figure 1 (Combs and Cooley, 1968; Rumberger, 1983; Natricello et al., 1986; Finn, 1989).

The conceptual model highlights causes that are outside the school system and causes which lie within the school system itself. This dichotomization, though simplistic, is meant essentially to clarify analysis and to guide policy options and recommendations. But, as we shall argue shortly, there are situations in which educational wastage results from the interaction of factors outside the school system and those within the school system. In such instances we shall label the causes of educational wastage as interactive; and this is a third dimension which needs to be added to the out of school and within school typology.

Specifically, the conceptual model depicted in Figure 1 posits that there are reciprocal relationships between factors related to community resources, community practices and family resources. All three are factors outside the school system. The second postulate is that each of the four out of school factors shown in the figure influence the three components of educational wastage either directly or indirectly through its operation on some of the within school factors. Thus, all the four out of school factors directly contribute to non-enrolment. This is persuasive since those who do not enroll are outside the direct sphere of influence of schools. Nonetheless, two factors within school, namely school resources (usually school places) and school practices, such as user charges, disciplinary policies and teacher behavior, may also inhibit children from enrolling in school.

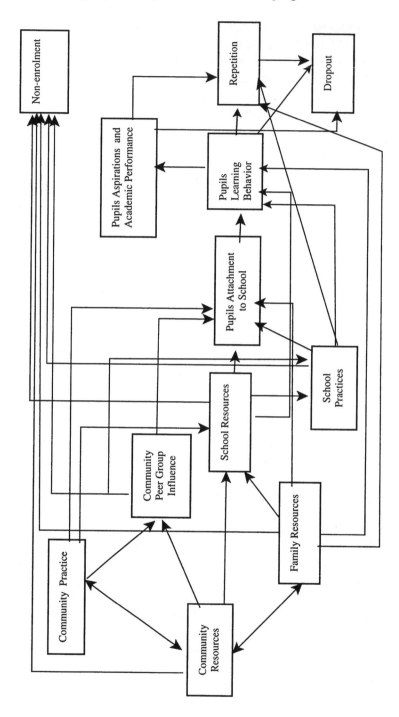

Figure 2.1 A Conceptual Model of Educational Wastage

The model suggests that out of school factors contribute to both repetition and dropout mainly through their impact on some of the within school factors. The only exception are factors included under family resources, which may also contribute directly to both repetition and dropout. For example, paucity of family financial resources may lead to interrupted learning and thus occasion repetition when funds become available or dropout where funds for schooling dry up. Community resources, community practices and family resources influence grade repetition and school dropout through their impact on school resources and pupil's feelings towards school, what is labeled in the figure as pupil's attachment to school. Furthermore, family resources influence school practices as well as pupils learning behavior. The later has an impact on pupil's aspirations and academic performance. Lastly, the factor labeled community peer group has a bearing on educational wastage. It is suggested that this out of school factor influences repetition and dropout aspects of wastage through its direct link to pupil's attachment to school and indirectly through pupil's learning behavior and pupil's aspirations and academic performance.

The impact of within school factors on educational wastage has been explained elaborately for repetition and dropout but only scantily for non-enrolment. According to the model depicted in Figure 1, school resources and school practices have a direct link to non-enrolment. Perhaps this link is not difficult to imagine. For example, school resources in the form of inadequate classroom space, fewer teaching personnel or insufficient number of schools in the face of great demand for schooling will result in practices such as multiple indirect user charges, harsh forms of discipline for pupils. These factors may discourage school enrolment on the part of some parents and children.

Finally, as the model illustrates, within school factors associated with school resources and practices, pupil's attachment to school, and their learning behavior (participation in school activities) all influence their educational and occupational aspirations and academic performance in school and hence decisions to repeat or drop out. Once pupils are enrolled in school, resources available in school influence repetition or dropout only indirectly through their influence on school practices (e.g. whether children are expelled for lack of school fees), pupil's attachment to school, pupil's learning behavior and their aspirations and academic performance.

It should be noted that both school practices and pupil's learning behavior (i.e. degree of participation in learning activities), could directly lead to decisions about grade repetition or dropping out from school. For instance, schools do make independent decisions about why some pupils should repeat grades and why some should quit school altogether. Likewise, the way pupils apply themselves to learning and related activities such as school rules, does select out who among them are candidates for either grade repetition or school delinkage.

The conceptual model also suggests a link between repetition and dropout. The research literature on educational wastage has documented that in a good number of cases pupils do drop out of school because they have low self-esteem (have low aspirations and expectations) and have poor academic track records (which includes frequent grade repetition) (Rumberger, 1983; Finn, 1989; Grissom and Shepard, 1989).

Finally, the model presented in Figure 1 suggests that educational wastage may be the result of the combined operation of out of school and within school factors. This may be the case where an out of school factor directly influences or interacts with and within school factor. In the model, the clear examples are the impact of community resources on school resources; of community practices on school resources, school practices and pupil's attachment to school; of community peer group on pupil's attachment to school; and the interaction of the family with virtually all within school factors.

A few practical examples should clarify the point we are trying to make here. Suppose children are unable to enroll in a particular school because community members are unwilling to contribute funds and labor to build more classrooms and that this is largely the result of poor relationships between the head teacher, teachers and parents. This would be a good example where children's inability to enroll in school is the result of poor school leadership and reluctant or hostile community leaders and members. It would be a good case in which non-enrolment has resulted from out of school and within school processes. Another good example of this interactive trajectory between out of school and within school factors is the case where parents strike a deal with teachers to have their academically fledgling children repeat an upper primary grade to improve their chances of passing a standardized national examination. This kind of repetition resulting from parent-teacher collaboration is a good example of the conjoint operation of out of school and within school factors to bring about educational wastage.

The conceptual model elaborated above is used below to review research related to educational wastage. In undertaking the literature review, we shall from time to time make reference to comparative literature to reinforce the point being made.

Review of Previous Studies on Educational Wastage

Wastage in primary school education is a pressing problem in Kenya. Non-enrolment and dropout are felt keenly in the poorer and also pastoralist sectors of Kenyan society. In contrast, repetition seems more of a common practice among children from better economically endowed regions and relatively more affluent parents whose educational aspirations for their children is high. But the available literature also ventures into some explanations of the three components of primary school wastage; non-enrolment, repetition and dropout.

The task in this part of the chapter is to present the evidence emanating in this literature about the correlates of non-enrolment, repetition and dropout. The presentation is guided as much as possible by the conceptual format outlined in the preceding section. Accordingly, the literature on non-enrolment, repetition and dropout are reviewed. The focus of the review is on the causes of the components of wastage. The independent as well as the joint causes are considered. We present sequentially in the sections, which follow each aspect of educational wastage in terms of the location of forces, which influence its occurrence.

It is to be noted that not all the works reviewed set out explicitly to study educational wastage. A number did, but quite many touched on issues related to educational wastage only incidentally. What they reveal about educational wastage is, nonetheless, informative and important.

Non-Enrolment

Causes Within School

In the main, it is possible to identify two within school factors which account for non-enrolment in primary schools in Kenya. The first of these two factors was broadly described as shortage of schools, paucity of school facilities such as classrooms and school resources such as textbooks and teaching personnel. A number of studies locate these problems predominantly in a number of heavily populated districts and urban centers where pre-schools were generally lacking and primary school places are too few to meet demand for schooling (Masariru, 1981; Cheptegei, 1982; Wafula, 1984; Onyango, 1986). Other studies mentioning this problem pointed out that in some regions of the country, particularly arid and semi-arid pastoralist ecological zones, not only were schools few but those available were generally located far from the children's houses (Chege, 1983). This problem of few schools or classes and other school resources was seen as resulting from inefficiency and insensitivity of the Ministry of Education and the school system generally.

The second within school factor, which contributed to non-enrolment, was given as the selective or preferential (biased) grade-one admission practices.   In some instances, attendance of pre-school was made a prerequisite for grade-one admission contrary to guidelines from the Ministry of Education. In some instances, the performance profile of children from a particular family was made a condition for the admission of their younger siblings.   In some cases, head teachers refused to admit children of the poor because it was perceived that their parents would be unable to afford user charges and so preferential admission went to children of rich parents (Cheptegei, 1982; Wafula, 1984).   This practice of preferential grade-one admission often results in failure by some children to enroll in school all together or in enrolment when they are beyond the official age and thus run the risk of dropping out subsequently.

Causes Out of School

As one would expect, most of the causes for failure by children to enroll in school lie outside the school system. The literature emphasized three major out of school causes of non-enrolment and mentioned two additional factors.

Parental and community poverty was mentioned as perhaps the leading cause of exclusion of children from schooling. It was pointed out that parental inability to pay for costs associated with participation in school resulted in non-enrolment (Masariru, 1981; Menya, 1992; Wamahiu, 1972). These researchers have also noted that when only meager financial resources could be made available, parental or guardian decisions to enroll in school favored male children over female children.

Wamahiu (1992) has attributed the exclusion of female children from schooling to a second factor, namely cultural practice, which undervalues women as a social category.   References to this point included such observations as girls will only benefit their husband's families.   Muslim parents do not want to give their daughters a western education.   Maasai culture emphasizes the chastity of girls and they fear that educating girls will make them migrate to towns and, while there, engage in prostitution (Chege, 1983; Porsi, 1988; Wamchia, 1988). According to Porsi (1988), not only do the cultures of many nomadic and pastoralist communities channel girls into early (child) marriage but also prevent first born sons from abandoning the more valued tradition of herding of cattle in favor of participation in schooling (Porsi, 1988).

Long distances to be covered in reporting to schools by pupils were mentioned as another important cause of non-enrolment. It was observed that not only are such distances taxing to young children but they also involve physical risks from hostile persons or dangerous wild animals (Achola, Shiundu and Oradho, 1991; UNICEF, 1992). While it is true that persons hostile to young people are to be found in virtually every community in Kenya, the risks of molestation are higher in situations such as those to be found in ASAL districts, where inter-community tensions have been lingering for a long time due to the prevalence of cattle rustling and unequal access to grazing grounds.

Two additional school causes of non-enrolment were mentioned in the literature. Migration of a large number of families with school age children into such already crowded cities as Nairobi, Mombassa and Kisumu was identified as a cause of non-enrolment (Mwangi, 1988). These newly arrived children add to the pool of candidates for whom no school places are available in the already over-stretched primary schools in the cities.

Instability within the family was found by Wamahiu (1992) to be a cause of non-enrolment in certain situations. For instance, among some Muslim polygamous families at the Kenya coast, fathers refrain from financing the education of their daughters by divorced wives. Young girls who find themselves in this situation end up without a benefactor to have them enrolled to obtain education. In this kind of situation children fail to enroll in school not directly because of poverty, but rather as a form of punishment against an estranged wife. The child becomes a victim and is likely to become illiterate because of family circumstances over which it has little or no control.

All the five out of school causes of non-enrolment arise essentially from the nature and fortunes of communities and of individual families within them. The conceptual model outlined in Figure 1 captures, and therefore predicts, these possible outcomes quite well. The conceptual model also draws attention to the potential for community and family factors, (i.e. out of school causes) to combine with a number of factors such as school resource base, school practices and the level of pupils' attachment to school (i.e. within school factors). These combined factors may contribute to non-enrolment in school. Our examination of the literature on educational wastage in Kenya did not come up with any study which found a combined contribution to non-enrolment by causes within school and causes out of school. In the next section, we present the causes of repetition suggested by the extant literature on wastage in education in Kenya.

Repetition

There were considerably more scholarly writings on repetition as a factor in educational wastage at the primary school level in Kenya than on non-enrolment. As causes of repetition, factors within the school have a preponderant role, either operating alone or in conjunction with out of school forces. Thus, from the surveyed literature on Kenya, some eight major within school causes of repetition in primary school education were identified as were a further nine factors that were common to the school and the community. In contrast, only four directly out of school causes of repetition were mentioned in the literature. In this section we present the identified within school causes of repetition leaving the subsequent sections for out of school and interactive causes of this aspect of educational wastage.

Causes Within School

Perhaps it should come as no surprise that a good number of within school causes of grade repetition (three) were linked directly to the national examination system. A further two each emanated from the nature of the curriculum and pedagogical practices, respectively. One cause was related to the nature of school administration.

One central point about the examination system raised in the literature was its very competitive nature. Instruction and learning at the primary school level in Kenya, it was emphasized, is strongly guided by the Kenya Certificate of Primary Education (KCPE) examination taken by pupils to mark the completion of the primary school cycle in grade eight. There is strong motivation among pupils, teachers and parents for learners to pass this examination since it is essentially an allocation mechanism into secondary school education and other popular post-primary school training programs.

Thus, giving evidence from carefully researched studies, a number of writers reported that often pupils in senior primary grades are persuaded or compelled by teachers to repeat in order to improve their likelihood of passing the KCPE examination (Eshiwani, 1984; Ngau, 1991). Some pupils make the decision to repeat in consultation with, and usually encouragement from, teachers to enable them to obtain the level of passing that will enhance their admission into quality secondary schools (King, 1974; Nkimyangi, 1980; Sifuna, 1989). In certain instances pupils seek repetition in different districts from those in which they initially sat for the KCPE examination. This is because marks required for entry into a secondary school of reasonable quality are much lower in these districts of refuge (Onyango, 1986; Eshiwani, Achola, Ole Sena, 1988). Particularly vulnerable to these kinds of pupil in-migration are arid and semi-arid districts which are officially classified as educationally disadvantaged. In general, admission to secondary schools in these districts is easier to obtain than secondary schools in the rest of the districts (Nungen, 1997).

The second examination related cause of repetition, and which is merely a variant of the first, is poor academic performance by primary school pupils. In the majority of cases, repetition is the result of failure to pass the KCPE examination and concomitant inability to obtain a secondary school place or, at least, a secondary school of desired quality. The pupil then repeats the final primary school grade to make a second, or even third, attempt at the KCPE examination (Nkimyangi, 1980; Sifuna, 1988). In other situations, schools make pupils repeat in lower grades of primary schools because of unsatisfactory academic work (Ngau, 1991; Aichi, 1992). This is how some schools penalize slow learners in an education system where remedial instruction is not part of education policy and is in consequence rarely given.

The third cause of grade repetition linked to examinations is a direct offshoot of unsatisfactory academic performance. The reviewed literature documents that situations exist where head teachers and teachers insist on grade repetition for pupils who are perceived as academically weak, to repeat grades. The intention is largely a selfish one in the sense that such pupils should not attempt the KCPE examination unless and until they are likely to obtain good scores to boost the school's comparative academic ranking nationally (Onyango, 1986). This strong orientation towards examinations and its concomitant valuation of relative national ranking on the KCPE examination, propels school to distort coverage of the official school curriculum in favor of only examinable content of the curriculum (King, 1974; Sifuna, 1988). The long-term consequence of this practice is that learners who terminate their schooling at the primary level and even those who enroll in further education fail to develop the skills of critical thinking and practical problem-solving capacities (Ahai, 1988). Two causes of repetition related to the characteristic of the curriculum are its broad and crowded content on the one hand, and English language medium of instruction on the other. Let us take each of these two in turn.

In the first instance, some researchers reported that repetition was blamed on a very broad, almost amorphous primary school curriculum. Typical views on this point took the form of statements such as 'there are too many subjects not all of which are desirable to students'. Or, 'that the 8-4-4 curriculum is too demanding for children of primary school age'. A few researchers have observed that the primary school curriculum demoralizes academically weak students or that the primary school cycle should be extended by additional two years. It was also mentioned that the curriculum is not only generally demanding but also particularly difficult for female pupils in the area of science and mathematics (King, 1974; Ngau, 1991; Achola, Shiundu, Orodho, 1992). The last mentioned point is of long standing dispute in both the primary and, especially, secondary school curricula. The perceived difficulty may largely be due to the abstract way science and mathematics are taught in Kenyan classrooms.

The second curriculum related source of repetition was reported to be the use of English as a medium of instruction right from lower primary school grades. Sifuna (1988) reports the existence of some confusion in language policy governing primary school education in the lower grades in the late 1960s. In rural areas, mother tongue and Kiswahili may be used in the first two grades, followed by the introduction of English from the third grade. In most urban schools, in contrast, the use of English starts immediately in the first grade.

The mother tongue is now used in the first three grades of primary schooling in rural areas with the introduction of some English from grade-one. Kiswahili is also taught from grade-one. In urban primary schools, Kiswahili serves as a substitute for mother tongue in the first three grades, except in areas such as the Kenyan Coast where it is the mother tongue at these grade levels. By the fourth grade, mother tongue is abandoned as a medium of instruction in favor of English, but Kiswahili continues to be taught alongside English up to the end of the primary school cycle in grade eight (and up to grade twelve for those who join secondary education). Many primary school teachers in fact treat the use of mother tongue for instruction in the first three grades of primary school as optional and use English instead.

Whatever the case, English is poorly understood by many primary school pupils. As a result, performance in this subject is generally poor in both lower and upper primary school classes. A few researchers report that poor performance is a cause of grade repetition. Some attribute poor performance on the part of pupils to poor knowledge of the English language by teachers and, as a result, to poor teaching of it within classrooms (Eshiwani, Achola, Ole Sena; 1988; Ngau, 1991). Since other subjects are taught and examined in English, a poor understanding of this language by teachers and pupils alike has alarming implications for learning in Kenyan primary schools.

Grade repetition which results from poor academic performance by pupils, may be traced to poor pedagogy. In this respect some of the studies reviewed point to grade repetition on poor teacher preparation. Either some primary school teachers were not trained for teaching at all, or their training was viewed to be of low quality. In consequence, such teachers lacked important pedagogical skills and were unable, therefore, to promote meaningful learning by pupils (Michieka, 1983; Kathuri, 1986). At times the poor instruction was compounded by a general lack of such basic school materials as textbooks, desks and chairs for pupils. Still in some instances, the source of inadequate learning was a shortage of teaching personnel and physical facilities such as classrooms and workshops (Eshiwani, 1984; Ngau, 1991).

Negative teacher attitudes and expectations were also mentioned among within school factors linked to poor pedagogy and hence to pupil academic failure and grade repetition. Low motivation among teachers and some head teachers was cited as a basis for failure by teachers to apply themselves to their work and to offer much needed assistance to slow learners (King, 1974; Eshiwani, Achola, Ole Sena, 1988). It is also reported in the literature that teachers, especially those with low morale, tend to have low academic expectations for their pupils. They simply do not believe in the ability of their pupils especially girls. Low teacher expectations do translate into low pupil academic performance and therefore to grade repetition (Egmose, 1981).

In the literature, low teacher morale is heavily attributed to poor terms of service, mainly in the form of low salaries and inhospitable working conditions. In Kenya the levels of teacher's salaries are negotiated between the Ministry of Education through the Teachers Service Commission (TSC) and the Kenya National Union of Teachers (KNUT). Working conditions in specific schools, however, can be made more or less tolerable by the administrative style of the head teacher. And it is in the latter realm that the eighth last within school cause of grade repetition in (primary) schools is wedged. This cause is broadly labeled as 'poor school administration'. Its manifestations mentioned in the literature include visible lack of discipline among pupils and teachers; lack of school-community linkages and, in many cases, school-community tensions.   Other manifestations are politically motivated teacher transfers at the behest of the head teacher (Michieka, 1983; Eshiwani, Achola, Ole Sena, 1988).

Causes Out of School

In addition to the foregoing eight within school causes of grade repetition, four out of school factors linked to this phenomenon emerged from the reviewed literature. These four causes have their trajectory in the community in general and the households in particular.

The first out of school factor in grade repetition was stated to be a strong preference by parents for quality secondary schools for their children. The results of this inclination include persuading children who could have joined middle range secondary schools and compelling head teachers to have such children repeat the final primary school grade and re-take the secondary school qualifying examination in order to obtain sufficiently high scores required to join the choicest secondary schools (Kirui, 1982; Kathuri, 1986). In Kenya, these are mainly some fourteen National Secondary Schools, although there are also approximately forty quality provincial and private secondary schools. It is understandable that most parents who exercise this leverage are politically well connected and or economically affluent.

Enrolment in primary schools by children who lacked pre-school or kindergarten exposure was the second household related cause of grade repetition.   Children without pre-school experience were reported to have great difficulty in adjusting to the group context that classroom learning involves.   This failure to adjust often resulted in poor learning and pupil repetition of lower grades at least (Nkimyangi, 1980; Wafula, 1984; Ngau, 1991). Generally this lack of pre-school exposure is the result of lack of pre-schools in communities or failure to take children to such schools partly on account of costs involved and partly because the Government has no policy which makes attendance at pre-school a prerequisite for admission to grade-one.

The third household related cause of grade repetition can be termed as small poor family environment. In the reviewed literature factors which were mentioned as causes of repetition and which can be subsumed under this rubric included alcoholism or drug addiction among parents, lack of household facilities for study at home, heavy family chores, encouragement of, or tolerance for, child marriages and indiscipline among children in the household (Briggs, 1973; Kirui, 1982; Achola and Shiunde, 1991). Often, these problems lead children to repeat a grade because they interrupt school attendance and take up time devoted to schoolwork. In fact, child marriages do not only result in grade repetition but also in school dropout.

The fourth and last out of school factor linked to grade repetition from the studies review was poor child nutrition and health. This is both a household and community problem. Poor nutrition and poor health tend to affect households in specific geographical contexts whether these are dry and therefore famine prone zones, areas exposed to endemic diseases or urban slums. It was pointed out that long absence from school due to ill-health results in missed learning. Similarly, children who are malnourished or hungry fail to learn well. All these were reported to lead to poor academic performance and therefore to result in grade repetition (Ngau, 1991; Michieka, 1983).

In the case of grade repetition, moreover, the reviewed literature revealed causes of this phenomenon, which arise from the conjoint influence of within school and out of school factors. In other words, there are instances when grade repetition results from the interaction of processes within the school system and outside the school. In the next section we give an account of these interactive factors as emerged from the examined literature on wastage in Kenya.

Interactive Factors

In the literature reviewed, there were quite a good number of these interactive causes of grade repetition. Eight broad categories were identified from the literature. These eight are explored sequentially in the paragraphs, which follow.

The first interactive cause of repetition passes by the appellate of poor motivation and support for learning. Included under its umbrella are such factors low motivation to learn on the part of children from low social status households and perceptions of few benefits to schooling on the part of such children (Nkimyangi, 1980; Eshiwani; 1984). School personnel usually reinforce the feelings of disadvantage that these children bring with them to school. For example, some teachers may regard learning difficulties experienced by poor children as a reflection of innate intellectual inability.

Also included under poor motivation and support for learning is the small amount of cooperation between a school and its surrounding community or the wider population of parents whose children attend a particular school.

The resulting tension between school personnel, mainly teachers, and community members which may include and other officials, usually creates a climate that is non-conducive to learning. The school may have little support in the form of physical facilities and learning resources; and pupils will have few people at home who can assist them with assigned school work (Eshiwani, Achola, Ole Sena, 1988; Achola, Shiundu and Orodho, 1992). In the short and long term, children operating under these kinds of conditions perform poor academic work which leads them to repeat a grade. As these children fall behind academically, they become frustrated and the likelihood of grade repetition increases (Cheptegei, 1982; Achola, Shiundu and Orodho, 1991).

A related component of poor motivation and support for learning which occasions grade repetition takes the form of lack of basic learning items or appropriate home condition for study. Often, some children attend school without accompanying basic learning resources like textbooks, mathematical sets, writing paper and pens. These children fail to do school work assigned to them because of poor conditions in their households (Briggs, 1973; Raju, 1973; Eshiwani, Achola, Ole Sena, 1988). The adverse conditions mentioned here lead to little learning, poor academic performance and grade repetition. The school authorities contribute to these conditions by failing to take action on children who come to school without the necessary learning items and who do not complete school work; and parents and other members of the household similarly fail to provide the learning resources and an environment where children can do homework.

Another source of motivation and support for learning is lack of appropriate role models in both the school and the community. Neither the community nor the school provides 'significant others' for the pupils to emulate and as a result, neither context stimulates the enthusiasm and curiosity needed for effective learning. There are in fact, instances when the cultural values of the school conflict with those of society, thereby precipitating confusion and ambivalence in learners (Cheptegei, 1982). Children faced with these conditions fail to do well in school and therefore tend to repeat grades.

The second interactive cause of grade repetition is mandatory payment of school levies. The levies may range from school fees, school uniforms and building fund to activity fees. Where the payment of levies is mandatory, children who do not pay according to prescribed time deadlines are usually released from school to secure the necessary funds. Those who stay away from school for long periods because of inability to obtain the funds miss valuable learning time. In some instances some children may be sent away from school a repeated number of times. These instances when children miss learning on account of being forced out for lack of payment of various levies are common in Kenyan primary schools and are reported to result in grade repetition (Eshiwani, 1984; Eshiwani, Achola, Ole Sena, 1988; Ngau, 1991).

A third interactive cause of grade repetition, which emerged from the reviewed literature, was actual or perceived lack of jobs and further educational opportunities for primary school pupils. It was reported that failure on the part of many primary school leavers to find meaningful employment or to proceed with higher education, led some primary school pupils to place less value in schooling. Put somewhat differently, primary schooling was seen as not necessarily a key to a better life (Nkimyangi, 1980; Cheptegei, 1982; Onyango, 1986).

It should be pointed out that failure to find employment after completion of primary school education reflects a combination of bad economic planning, imparting of an irrelevant school curriculum or inadequate coverage of relevant school curriculum. Whatever the case, the problem is as much due to factors in other sectors of society as it is due to factors in the educational system and educational practice in particular. In this respect, children repeat because of weak performance in school-specific and national examinations.

A related, and fourth interactive cause of grade repetition, was identified as loss of learning time on account of regular absence from school by some teachers. In some schools at long distances away from district educational offices, teachers find it difficult to attend to official matters that affect them promptly. As a result, some spend several days at the district offices in pursuit of solutions to personal problems such as the collection of salaries, requests for transfers or for promotion (Eshiwani, Achola, Ole sena, 1988). Furthermore, there were instances when many teachers habitually arrived in school late. This constituted some loss of learning time for pupils. Loss of learning time due to regular absence on the part of teachers, reflects an internal leadership laxity within the school, as well as external poor supervision by local level educational officials, community leaders and parents. In other words, factors within the school and outside the school are equally to blame for this situation.

Indiscipline among pupils in and outside school was mentioned as another cause of grade repetition. Problems of indiscipline among pupils included infrequent school attendance for unknown reasons, drug and alcohol consumption, engaging in petty trading activities which compete with school work, pupil violence and teenage sex and attendant pregnancy (Nkimyangi, 1980; Okume, 1992; Achola, Shiundu, Orodho, 1992). Pupils who engage in these kinds of activities miss learning either due to their own absence or because they are suspended from school for days as a disciplinary measure. It should be noted that many of the problems mentioned here arise from failure of the household and the school to instill appropriate behavior in the children. What the family and the school fail to do becomes mutually reinforcing and decidedly inimical to effective learning.

The location of schools at distances considered too far for pupils was mentioned as another cause of repetition. This is the sixth interactive cause of grade repetition in this review. The location of schools is influenced by the communities and the sanctioning authority in the Ministry of Education and its organs. The way children whose homes are located far from school are managed depends in large measure on the head teacher and his/her administrative practices. Such children can be temporarily accommodated within the school, they can be given special lessons to compensate for missed classes, or they can be denied any special attention. Additionally, parents can be prevailed upon to give such children some food to bring with them to school and/or to ensure that such children travel safely and as conveniently as possible to school. In a fundamental way, then, the issue of children having to travel far to school is both a school and a community (out of school) problem (Eshiwani, Achola, Ole Sena, 1988; Achola, Shiundu, Orodho, 1992). Long distances to school was highlighted as a major problem in sparsely settled areas such as arid and semi-arid lands (ASALs), and among urban slum children who must of necessity seek schools located away from their poor neighborhoods.

The other factor, and our seventh interactive cause, related to grade repetition is parental transfers to new work stations or/and the transfer of children to new schools. It was reported in the literature that schools do not have policy guidelines regarding times of the school calendar year during which they can accept transferring pupils, or the grade levels when such transfers are acceptable. As a result, transfers can in principle be processed at any time and for any grade at times because of pressure from influential parents. Pupils who transfer to a new school require more time to adjust to the new setting before they can start on the task of learning. This is particularly the case when they transfer into a school that is more achievement oriented than the ones from which they came. Because of the lack of clear policy governing transfers in Kenyan (primary) schools, a good number of pupils have adjustment problems, perform poorly and repeat a grade as a result (Michieka, 1983; Ngau, 1991).

The eighth, and last, interactive cause of grade repetition is purposeful withholding of pupils in a grade. This was common in senior primary school grades, particularly grades 7 and 8. Two reasons were cited for this practice. First, a desire by some parents that their children should be admitted to specific elite secondary schools; and second, a more widespread desire that by repeating, the children will obtain better examination scores to guarantee admission to acceptable, though not necessarily elite, secondary schools. At the same time, head teachers and teachers too, make some children repeat senior primary school grades to enhance the mean school score and therefore the schools national as well as district ranking in the Kenya Certificate of Primary Education (KCPE). In the majority of cases, repetition in the hope of better performance in the KCPE involves the active collaboration of pupils, their parents, communities and teachers (King, 1974; Nkimyangi, 1980; Ngau, 1991). It is this collaborative nature of the practice that earns it the term 'purposeful withholding or repetition'.

The review of literature undertaken up to this point has revealed a range of factors, mainly within school and jointly within and out of school, that cause repetition more than non-enrolment. This should, perhaps, not be unexpected since traditionally, conceptualization of educational wastage has not incorporated non-enrolment within its ambit. As was reported in the earlier sections of this chapter, the conventional conceptualization of wastage has tended to include only grade repetition and school dropout. We document next that, to a considerable degree, the causes of school dropout in Kenya are comparable to those for grade repetition.

Causes of School Dropout

From the reviewed literature it does appear that in the Kenyan case the causes of dropout from school are located outside the schools and in the interaction of processes within school and outside it, presumably in the wider community. In this section, school causes of dropout from primary schooling are identified along with five interactive causes. Strictly speaking only four within school causes of termination of primary schooling are identified. However, there are eight identifiable within school causes of grade repetition. The number of causes of school dropout which lie outside the school, is about double the number of causes of repetition. What all this amounts to is that, for Kenya at least, the preponderant number of causes of grade repetition in one way or another have their trajectory within the school system, whereas most of the causes of school dropout have their loco operandi in the community, i.e. outside the school system. In the next section, we give an account of the various causes of school dropout as identified in the literature in terms of within school, out of school and interactive factors.

Causes Within School

A number of the investigators, whose works are reviewed here, identified parental and community poverty as an underlying cause of dropout from school on the part of some pupils. It was pointed out that where parents lack the means to pay for such school charges like building funds, activity fees and uniforms, their children are compelled to quit school. The same fate befalls children whose parents cannot foot the costs of learning materials such as textbooks, exercise books, mathematical instruments, pens and pencils (Michieka, 1983; Ngau, 1991). Often, children who lack learning materials dropout of school due to some sense of shame arising from a feeling of relative deprivation, or they may actually be expelled from school by authorities.

The second school specific cause of dropout was given as lack of basic physical facilities and other teaching resources in some schools. Although the presence of these conditions may lead some children to dropout on their own initiative, many dropout only when the conditions precipitate poor academic performance (Michieka, 1983; Ngau, 1991). It has been long recognized that lack of critical learning resources such as trained teachers, appropriate and adequate classrooms, desks and chairs for pupils, textbooks for both teachers and pupils, impede effective teaching and learning resulting in poor academic performance by pupils (Eshiwani, Achola, Ole Sena, 1988; Shiundu and Achola, 1994).

The third within school cause of dropout was identified as poor social climate. By this is meant the extent to which the social organization of the school promoted or hampered learning by pupils. Poor school climate took different forms. For instance, some children found the learning process boring and therefore dropped out of school because of lack of interest (Achola, Shiundu, Orodho, 1991; Abagi, 1993). Usually, many of the children who drop out of school because of lack of interest are from low socio-economic status families whose low self-concept and educational expectations are further negatively reinforced by the teachers. Indeed some of the literature reported instances where open hostility by teachers to some pupils led to their dropping out of school (Raju, 1973; Wamahiu, 1992). Poor school climate has a more devastating impact on female pupils who tend to drop out more due to this situation than do male pupils.

The fourth cause of dropout emanating from the school was reported to be unacceptable behavior by pupils, which results in their suspension and, ultimately, expulsion from school. Thus, some pupils are expelled from school for breaking school rules related to proper conduct. Examples are children who behave rudely to teachers, those who frequently miss attending school or who fall under the influence of drugs or alcohol during school hours (Michieka, 1983; Achola, Shiundu, Orodho, 1991; Abagi, 1993). Many school systems in Kenya are not adequately sensitized and empowered to guide and counsel children with behavior difficulties. Periodic suspension and subsequent expulsion of such children from school is the more common practice.

Having outlined the four within school causes of dropout from school, we give an account in the next section of the causes of this phenomenon that are located outside the school. According to the reviewed literature on educational wastage in Kenya, most of the factors which lead to dropout from school are to be found outside the school. In the final part of this section on dropout, we shall show, moreover, that many of the out of school causes of dropout interact with some within school factors to result in the problem of dropout.

Causes Out of School

As is to be expected many of the immediate causes of school dropout outside the school's sphere of influence were located within the households, particularly the immediate family, and within the general community. The rest appeared to have a wider geographical focus than the immediate community.

Three family-specific causes of dropout mentioned in the literature are poor household facilities for study, burdening many school going children with household chores and withdrawal of children from school due to involvement in gaining supplementary family income. Although both problems appear linked to parental poverty, they were mentioned in the literature as more or less problems that were specific to the family.

It was pointed out that some pupils drop out of school out of frustration arising from their failure to do school work at home because of lack of rooms for study, poor lighting, and overcrowded and noisy living conditions (Raju, 1973; Eshiwani, Achola, Ole Sena, 1988; Achola and Shiundu, 1991; Ngau, 1991). Where children affected in this way do not voluntarily leave school, they are subsequently forced out through pressure from school authorities on account of poor academic record.

The second reason for dropout from school, and one still linked to the family, was identified as the involvement of children in household chores. It was observed that some families seem to have little value for education as manifested in their tendency to give children, especially girls, heavy household chores or to withdraw them from school to become 'caregivers' for younger siblings or even elderly members of the household (Briggs, 1973; Ngau, 1991; Eshiwani, 1984; Okumu, 1992). Clearly, a heavy involvement in household chores by children who also attend school considerably reduces the time they have for study and has an adverse effect on their academic output and record. Eventually this poor academic record may compel them to drop out or to be forced out.

The use of children's labor in wage employment or income generation of some kind was a further family-specific cause of school dropout. It was reported by some of the investigators that some parents, particularly poor ones, encouraged and at times forced their children to engage in income-earning activities in order to supplement household incomes. Such activities included petty trading and wage employment. Children involved in income generating activities eventually experienced great difficulties in coping with schoolwork and had to subsequently dropout or be withdrawn by their parent, from school (Nkimyangi, 1980; Michieka, 1983; Ngau, 1991; Okumu, 1992).

A fourth cause of school dropout was the awareness by many community members of lack of employment opportunities for those who complete primary schooling. This existence of widespread unemployment among primary school leavers, strengthened the resolve of parents in communities whose orientations to Western education were weak or even hostile to begin with, to remove their children from school. While some poor parents were also prone to this practice, it was more common among parents in communities, such as those of pastoralists and Muslims, which have traditionally resisted Western education (Chaptegei, 1982;Michieka, 1983).

This withdrawal of children from school because of perceptions of education as of little economic value, is closely related to situations reported earlier regarding the involvement of children in performing household chores or participating in income generating activities. In the arid and semi-arid parts of the country, children are usually withdrawn from school to look after cattle owned by the adult members of the household and, in the case of girls to attend to such domestic chores as fetching water and firewood and taking care of younger children in the household. Among poor parents in many parts of the country, children may be withdrawn from school to undertake wage employment. Girls from these poor households usually end up in the country's larger urban centers as house girls in middle and upper income families. In other words, child labor is one cause of dropout by a good number of children from the primary school system.

Cultural beliefs and practices in some communities were identified as another cause of school dropout. This fifth factor is of critical importance in the early withdrawal of children from school in many pastoralist and nomadic communities as well in areas that profess the Islamic faith. These communities and families have in common suspicions about the negative influences of Western education on their children. In many of these communities, the custom is to assign girls exclusively reproductive and household roles. Western education is perceived to delay the onset of reproductive roles as well as the productive role as housewives whose labor is meant to benefit the husband and his offspring. Early marriages, in fact child marriages, are therefore common for girls in these communities (Chege, 1983; Wamahiu, 1988; Achola and Shiundu, 1991).

In these communities, and others, there are cultural practices related to right of passage which conflict with continued school attendance by pupils who have undergone the customary ceremonies. Examples are circumcision and moranism, and in some communities female circumcision. These ceremonies signal the start of adulthood and are at variance with continued schooling where a man or a woman would continue to be a pupil which is considered to be a non-adult role (Chege, 1983; Eshiwani, Achola, Ole Sena, 1988; Porsi, 1988).

Another factor which was identified as a cause of dropout from school, and this the sixth, was poor health and lack of proper health care for some pupils. A number of the studies reviewed here reported that some children who had prematurely left school cited illness and poor health as the reason for their dropping out. Poor health among pupils was more widespread in areas with endemic diseases such as malaria and bilhazia infection and among the physically handicapped pupils (Michieka, 1983; Achola and Shiundu, 1991; Ngau, 1991). The condition of unhealthy school children is difficult to improve since many rural schools are located far from any health facilities while these facilities are also generally inaccessible to children in urban slums who need health services most (Okumu, 1992).

Surveys of primary schools in seven UNICEF supported districts in Kenya, under the Household Welfare Monitoring and Evaluation Survey Program confirmed that many rural schools lack access to health facilities. Another survey of primary schools in Nairobi, Mombassa and Kisumi, showed that schools located in urban slums had less access to health facilities and services than schools in middle and upper socio-economic neighborhoods (Okumu, 1992).

The final out of school factor related to dropout from school is inter-community conflicts. Conflicts in the form of armed clashes and at times large scale warfare were reported to occur between some ethnic groups, especially in arid and semi-arid districts over such resources as livestock and access to grazing lands. The general atmosphere of insecurity that these ethnic conflicts engender, lead to many children in the affected communities withdrawing from school since their security cannot be guaranteed (Eshiwani, Achola, Ole Sena, 1988; Achola and Shiundu, 1991; Achola, Shiundu, Orodho, 1991).

In the final section on dropout, we outline interactive factors which were identified as causes of dropout from school. The factors are interactive in the sense that within school and out of school processes operate together to push children out of school.

Interactive Causes

To reiterate a point made earlier, some five interactive causes of dropout from school were identified in the reviewed literature. Unlike the case of grade repetition, the five interactive causes of dropout from school are distinct from one another. We examine these five next.

The first interactive causes of dropout from school was given as parental or guardian inability to afford the costs associated with schooling. School systems themselves contribute to this problem in Kenya by proliferating the number and levels of levies required of the children. In public primary schools in Kenya, the official government position is that no school fees are charged. In spite of this official policy, schools do levy such charges as building funds, activities fees, parents-teachers association (PTA) funds and funds for school uniforms. Some school systems collect huge sums of money from these levies since the amounts which may be levied have not been standardized by the government. The reviewed literature revealed that many children from pastoralist communities and from poor parents in both rural and urban areas dropout of school because they are unable to pay the various levies (Nkimyangi, 1980; Meme, 1987; Ngau, 1991; Achola and Shiundu, 19991).

The second factor mentioned as a cause of dropout was irrelevant primary school curriculum to the needs and interests of some communities. This irrelevance took several forms. It was claimed for instance that what is regarded as cultural resistance to schooling is in fact evidence of lack of linkage between education and cherished community values and practices. Another aspect of this problem is that what schools teach is regarded as of little use for life after school (Kiriu, 1982; Achola, Shiundu and Orodho, 1991; Abagi, 1993). The question here is one of a relevant curriculum and lack of such relevance implies failure by the school system to adapt to the needs and interests of the community and of community leaders to actively seek consultations with educational authorities. Instead, both sides tend to react with hostility to each other or with uneasy aloofness (Nguru, 1980; Nkimyangi, 1980; Eshiwani, Achola, Ole Sena, 1988).

Pregnancy among female pupils was a third interactive factor linked to school dropout. The problem affected girls in upper primary grades. Teenage pregnancy may reflect inadequate supervision and guidance on the part of the family as well as the schools which teenagers attend (Eshiwani 1984; Gitau 1985; Nderitu, 1987). Termination of schooling for girls who become pregnant is a school matter and reflects a costly educational policy that fails to give girls a second chance. Thus, both the family and school contribute in various ways to dropout from school by girls on account of pregnancy. The family and the school fail to give girls proper guidance and counseling to sexually active teenagers and as a result, a number of teenaged girls end up pregnant. The schools then turn around and expel the pregnant girls from school.

Dropout from school was also attributed to long distances children have to cover to reach school. It was reported that some children decide to quit school because they are unable to handle the long distances they have to walk to school. This problem was regarded as particularly severe in the arid and semi-arid parts of the country occupied mainly by pastoralist communities. These are large areas of sparse settlement which make proper school mapping very difficult (Michieka, 1983).

The fifth and last interactive reason for school dropout, which emerged from the literature, was failure by some teachers to accept postings in schools located in remote areas of the country. Such places are regarded by many teachers as hardship areas. It was reported that many teachers regard assignment to work in remote areas as punishment. Trained teachers in particular tend to refuse assignment for work in remote areas. The situation is usually aggravated by the fact that many teachers are not indigenous to the remote areas where they teach or are expected to teach. As a result, there tends to be high turnover of teaching staff in these areas, and where the desire to leave is frustrated, teachers affected suffer from low morale (Eshiwani, Achola, Ole Sena, 1988; Porsi, 1988; Achola, Shiundu and Orodho, 1991).

The reluctance of some teachers to work in remote areas is often the result of perceived poor reception by such communities, lack of support by the community leaders and even parents and lack of the provision of appropriate incentives by educational authorities. The problem, therefore, arises from both the communities and the school system itself.

3   Primary School Wastage Among Special Groups

Introduction

In our discussion up to this point about wastage in education, the question of wastage for whom has not been addressed directly. In Chapter 1, we underscored the importance of formal education for individuals and groups. The privacy of place given to formal education links up aptly with the issue of which groups acutely experience any one or all three forms of educational wastage. Stated perhaps more pointedly, there would be no point to invest time, effort and resources in a discussion of educational wastage if education was in fact an activity of little or no value.

We argued the point in Chapter 1 that acquisition of formal education is important in at least two fundamental respects. First, as a direct avenue for the acquisition of literacy in its widest sense, which includes the skills of reading, writing and computation. Such literacy is the basis for accumulation of knowledge and its utilization. An individual without meaningful literacy skills is denied the wider range of information and its application that literacy makes possible.

Second, formal education is an important yardstick by which many contemporary societies, including Kenya, allocate individuals into occupational and related social roles. In new and less industrialized countries such as Kenya the link between the level of education completed and occupational status or level is stronger than in the old and more industrialized countries. It is this real or perceived relationship between formal education and occupational status and ultimately social status that makes the demand for education particularly strong and widespread in Kenya. Groups and persons with little or no access to formal education are, *ipso facto*, regarded to suffer distinct disadvantage in terms of participation in the key public roles of society.

Since exclusion or restriction from participation in formal education results in inequities in allocation to key roles in society, discussion of wastage in education is at the core of the concern for equity. It is therefore necessary to provide an understanding of equity in education and to highlight the sense in which educational equity is perceived in official circles in Kenya. This helps us to identify groups that in the Kenyan context have historically been disadvantaged in access to and participation in formal education. We turn to these issues in the subsequent sections.

Understanding Educational Equity

There has been a strong tendency to confuse equity with equality. We hope to show that while the two concepts may be related, they are different. Let us start with an explication of meaning, which has been assigned to the concept of educational equity.

At the core, educational equity is concerned with extent to which given social groups are fairly or unfairly represented in schooling. The concept of equity in education refers to whether given groups are adequately represented among pupils, teachers, educational officials or some other category, relative to the size of these social groups in the total population of which they are subsets. For a valued resource such as education, the tendency for its distribution is to be skewed, with some groups being over represented and other groups being under represented. Equity has conventionally been determined in education by using a measure called Representative Index (RI). This measure of equity is calculated as follows (Dutta, 1984).

$$\text{Representative Index} = \frac{\text{Percentage of group X members in given resource at time (t)}}{\text{Percentage of group X members in total population at time (t)}}$$

When the Representative Index is equal to 1, a group is equitably (justly) represented in a given resource. A group is under represented where the Representative Index is less than 1 and over represented where the index is larger than 1. If full equity were attainable, then all groups in a composite population would have a representative index equal to one in terms of their share of a particular resource.

Confusion between the concepts of educational equity and educational equality became compounded with the publication of the book Equality of Educational Opportunity (Coleman, 1966). Coleman's work mapped the structure of educational inequalities between racial and socio-economic groups and factors accounting for such inequalities in the United

States of America. The title of the book itself suggested a desire for equality in access (opportunity) to education among the groups Coleman identifies (Harvey and Noble, 1985; Harvey and Klein, 1989; Murphy and Gipps, 1996).

Equality implies lack of differences between groups with regard to access, utilization and outcome related to a given resource. It means equal proportions in terms of access, participation, retention and performance in education. A simple example will suffice. Suppose that a dominant group A in society, say in terms of the number of its members who use a particular resource, say primary school education, constitutes 70 percent of this group in society. Suppose two other groups, B and C also use this resource. Equality principle will demand that groups B and C also have 70 percent of their membership use the same resource as does 70 percent of the membership of the dominant group A. Thus, equality is achieved because identical proportions of otherwise numerically different groups A, B and C have access to the resource in contention. The numbers of persons from the three groups that have access to the resource cannot be equal because the three groups are unequal in size to begin with.

It is from the premise of inherent differences in sizes of groups that equity considerations come into play. The size of each group as a share of the aggregate population of all groups is taken into account and is compared with the share of each group in reference to the resource of interest. The Representative Index mentioned in the preceding paragraphs gives the relative representativeness of each group. By comparing the indices across groups, one can discern groups which are under represented (indices below 1), which groups are fairly represented (indices of 1 or close to 1), and which groups are over represented (indices clearly above 1). In brief, equity adjusts for the fact that groups involved in a valued resource are of unequal sizes in the wider population and it is the proportional (or relative) differences in the group's share of the resource under consideration.

Equity is thus premised on distributive justice which equality is not consistently concerned about. The two concepts may dovetail into a common meaning where it is possible to provide everyone with a specific desired resource. In this case, representative indices on the particular resource for all groups would be unity (1). Since in many instances it is difficult to provide a given resource to everyone in practice, equity and equality hardly mesh.

While equity focuses on the degree of fairness in access, participation, performance and outcome, how to bring about such fairness in representation of various groups is a controversial point. Usually, three strategies are used to adjust the level of representation for disadvantaged groups. These strategies are a) Assigning quotas to specific groups in an attempt to increase their representation; b) Providing the under represented groups with more resources (such as remedial instruction in education) to improve their competitive capacity and, as a result, their representation; c) Increasing the representation of under represented groups by applying less stringent criteria in admission and thus paying little attention to quality concerns.

The second and third measures are mutually exclusive; but either may be applied in combination with the first measure. Essentially, all three are policy measures, which a country's leadership has to weigh and make a decision about if equity among certain groups in the particular country is regarded as a desirable goal.

Our concern with educational wastage among a variety of social groups in Kenya rests on the fact that the Kenyan political leadership has made educational equity an important aspect of educational policy. This point was presented at length in chapter 1. It may suffice here to reiterate that on the eve of political independence, the leading political party, the Kenya African National Union (KANU) pledged to provide universal basic education once political independence was obtained. Various constraints, mainly economic, prevented the implementation of this pledge. At the start of the 1990-decade, this issue was revisited, largely with prompting from such international donor agencies as UNICEF, UNESCO, UNDP and the World Bank. First, Kenya joined many other countries of the world in endorsing the goals of the World Conference on Education for All (WCEFA) held in March of 1990 in Jomtien, Thailand. The provision of (basic) education for every child and adult who had missed out on schooling and were as a result illiterate was a crucial goal. Second, later that same year in September, Kenya was again among those countries that endorsed the World Declaration of the Rights of the Child in New York City. Among the basic rights of the child was the right to receive basic education. On this point, the New York Summit on The Rights of the Child essentially re-affirmed the UN Declaration of Human Rights. But the major departure in New York was that countries such as Kenya, which had so far maintained a studious ambivalence, openly declared a readiness to implement the policy pledging the provision of education to every child.

Pledges are always made about an issue because a gap exists between the actual and the desired or even the expected. Kenyan authorities continue to make promises about providing every child and adult with basic education.

To identify which groups have lagged behind in terms of basic education coverage, it is necessary to provide some documented evidence. We attach the label special to these groups principally because they require special attention to bring them into mainstream education system. We devote the rest of this chapter to a discussion of these special groups.

Educational Wastage Among Special Groups

In terms of wastage in education, certain social groups are normally identified to be particularly vulnerable. In a wide variety of national and even local contexts, these groups usually include girls or women, racial and ethnic minorities, people in certain religious denominations or sects, poor people and their children, the physically and mentally challenged (handicapped) and people in especially difficult circumstances such as those, mainly children, in refugee camps or those who are orphans whether as a result of war or natural causes. The task in the rest of this chapter is to determine whether or not in the Kenyan context these are the same groups, which experience educational wastage.

To start with, in many African countries the under representation of females in primary school education, and all levels of education for that matter, started with the establishment of schools by missionaries. This sex disparity in school enrolment and attendance became pronounced throughout the period of colonial rule. Kenya reflected this colonial pattern. For instance, at the end of colonial rule in 1963, about 70 percent of boys and only 41 percent of girls among children aged 7-10 years were enrolled in lower primary school classes (grades 1 to 4); and 58 percent of boys and a meager 21 percent of girls among children aged 11-14 years were enrolled in upper primary school standards (grades 5 to 7) (Thias and Carnoy, 1972).

The first post-independence government of the late President Kenyatta and the second regime of President Moi devoted considerable effort to increasing the enrolment of girls in primary school education. These efforts were successful to an extent. However, the basic patterns in gender disparities reported by Thias and Carnoy (1972) for the early years of independence have persisted to a large extent.

For instance, in studies of retention patterns in primary schools in seven districts supported by UNICEF in the early 1990s, it was found that in many cases less than one half of standard 1 cohort in a district reached standard eight. The UNICEF studies titled 'Household Welfare and

Monitoring Evaluation Surveys' were conducted between 1990 and 1992 in the districts of Kisumu, Baringo, South Nyanza, Embu, Kitui, Kwale and Mombassa. The situation found in Baringo district and the then South Nyanza district was quite typical of the general scene. The primary school completion rates in 1990 for those who had joined grade 1 in 1983 were 43 percent in Baringo and 29 percent in South Nyanza. In terms of gender for these grade 1 cohorts, 40 percent of the boys compared to 40 percent of the girls in Baringo completed grade eight. Comparable figures for South Nyanza were 33 percent of the boys and only 24 percent of the girls who completed primary schooling (UNICEF, 1992).

It is plausible, even possible, that some of the pupils transferred to other schools outside the original district in which they had enrolled. Nonetheless, the fact that much fewer girls than boys survived to standard eight, suggests that in fact most of the pupils dropped out of school. Most primary schools in the country are non-boarding institutions and many parents are generally reluctant to send children, particularly girls, far from home for primary school education essentially because of the uncertainties involved.

Furthermore, evidence from a number of micro-surveys of dropout levels by gender in Kenya report findings, which consistently confirm higher rates for girls than boys. These studies show, in fact, that girls are particularly susceptible to dropping out in the upper primary school grades (Kiriu, 1982; Okumu, 1982; Gitau, 1985; Meme, 1987; Nderitu, 1987; Ngau, 1991). In Table 3.1 we report retention patterns for four different grade 1 cohorts that reached various grades in primary school. The results confirm that higher dropout rates for girls in upper primary school grades are true irrespective of the social status of the school.

Table 3.1 Four Standard 1 Cohorts Reaching Given Grade Levels by Type of School

School Type and Pupil's Gender	Grade Reached by Cohorts			
	8* (1986-93) No. (Percent)	7** (1987-93) No.(Percent)	6 (1988-93) No.(Percent)	5 (1989-93) No.(Percent)
Slum Schools				
Male	296 (105.7)	300(94.9)	316(95.2)	377(116.4)
Female	235 (60.1)	352(78.9)	394(128.8)	404(107.2)
Middle Schools				
Male	352(88.4)	368(2.2)	371(82.8)	381(86.4)
Female	321(81.9)	332(3.2)	353(93.9)	332(83.8)
Affluent Schools				
Male	402(104.1)	380(9.6)	455(102.5)	425(94.9)
Female	366(74.8)	360(102.3)	437(106.3)	414(102.0)

*The proportions shown at this level give a crude measure of primary school competition rates.
**The proportions reaching these lower grades give a measure of retention rates. Percentages above 100 reflect transfers and repetition at the grade levels.

The figures indicate that in grades 7 and 8, smaller proportions of girls than boys are retained in school. Below grade 7, the proportions of girls and boys that remain in school are either about the same or those for girls are higher than for boys. These patterns do not, however, contradict other results reported by similar micro-studies that have been already cited, to the effect that more girls than boys dropout of primary schools.

In a study of primary school wastage conducted by the Bureau of Educational Research (BER) at Kenyatta University for the Ministry of Education, various educational personnel were asked to identify groups they perceived to be most affected by wastage. Almost without exception, teachers, head teachers, local educational officers and head office education officers stated that girls are more adversely affected by non-enrolment and dropout than are boys. On the other hand, repetition was more of a problem for boys than for girls.

We can conclude this section with the statement that whether looked at from the national or district level, or from micro-surveys of a few school systems, girls constitute a visible category of those groups that require special attention to enhance their participation in schooling and related literacy programs.

We examine next whether or not in the Kenyan situation a case can be made today about the existence of ethnic groups or communities that only marginally participate in primary schooling. It is known that in Kenya, as in a number of other African countries, the establishment and growth of schools during colonial rule was not even for all parts of the country. On attainment of political independence, a number of African countries made efforts to redress the inherited regional educational imbalances. Kenya's efforts in this direction during the regime of President Kenyatta (1963-1978) were half-hearted and uncoordinated. Many of the country's 5-year development plans kept referring to this issue without specific strategies on how to resolve regional education disparities and disadvantages. Subsequent comments on education after the Kenyatta era drew attention to the widening education imbalances.   The result was that areas which had an earlier lead in participation in schooling, maintained and consolidated this advantage.

Bolder efforts to address educational imbalances were made under the regime of President Moi, who had assumed leadership of Kenya after the death of Kenyatta in late August 1978. President Moi introduced a number of measures to increase the participation in schooling of children from disadvantaged regions. Most important among these were the provision of milk and lunch in schools located in educationally disadvantaged districts. These measures have increased school enrolment for children in disadvantaged regions of the country, but without necessarily appreciably narrowing the gap in enrolment trends for pupils in many historically educationally advantaged regions.

Information provided in Table 3.2 points to the continued relative disadvantage in primary school enrolments for districts in the Coast Province, the arid and semi-arid lands (ASALs) in North Eastern and Rift Valley Provinces.   These are the very same provinces in Kenya, which have historically low enrolment levels in schools.

Subject to the normal pitfalls of censuses data, the table presents estimates of characteristics of whole populations. This suggests that they give a more complete and accurate picture of the situation than would sample surveys. And because what the data reflect are structural problems, the patterns are unlikely to change radically in the medium term (say periods of 10 to 15 years).

The patterns reflected in the table enable us to at least resolve three issues. First, the data reveal that areas with the lowest female literacy rates (rates less than 50 percent) are also the ones which record the lowest primary school enrolment rates and especially among girls. All these areas are districts located in the historically educationally disadvantaged Coast Province North-Eastern Province and the semi-arid and arid parts of Eastern and Rift Valley Provinces.

The 14 districts shown in Table 3.3 constitute the critical zones of the country where the problem of educational wastage, in the form of non-enrolment and dropout in particular, is most acute. They all have primary school enrolment rates for both boys and girls that are well below the national averages for 1989. In the study conducted by the Bureau of Education Research at Kenyatta University for the Ministry of Education, headquarters Ministry of Education offices overwhelmingly concurred that non-enrolment in and dropout from primary school affected mainly children from communities in the arid and semi-arid districts of the country. The arid and semi-arid districts these officers had in mind include the 14 districts listed above.

The second point we can resolve from the patterns reflected in Tables 3.2 and 3.3, is the political economy of the groups, which inhabit most of the educationally disadvantaged districts. The dominant communities, which reside in eleven of the thirteen districts, are heavily involved in a pastoralist economy. In other words, a pastoralist economy, because of its inherently nomadic life style, places children in an unstable condition regarding school attendance. Looking after cattle and frequent movements by families in search of grazing lands make it impossible to participate in learning arrangements which rely on sedentary school classrooms.

Table 3.2   Primary School Participation Rates by Gender and District*

District	Male in school	P.R**	Female in school	P.R
A. Female literacy 80% and above				
Nairobi	73,386	73.9	80,272	73.7
Kiambu	89,747	78.4	91,287	78.9
Nyeri	64,738	77.3	65,424	79.0
Nyandarua	37,562	74.9	37,461	76.5
B. Female literacy 70-79%				
Bungoma	61,209	65.9	64,563	68.5
Embu	35,582	67.6	36,431	69.9
Kirinyaga	39,086	71.9	39,653	74.1
Kisii	119,602	70.7	121,680	72.0
Laikipia	21,703	71.1	20,817	70.8
Machakos	136,250	67.9	138,712	70.3
Mombassa	27,867	68.8	28,429	67.6
Muranga	97,703	77.0	97,305	78.3
Nakuru	84,360	74.3	83,915	74.9
Taita-Taveta	18,971	67.1	19,325	69.1
Uasin Gishu	39,917	69.5	41,138	71.3
C. Female literacy 60-69%				
Elgeyo-Marakwet	22,233	75.7	22,163	75.8
Kakamega	136,881	66.4	143,107	68.9
Kericho	88,765	70.9	91,233	73.2
Kisumu	63,980	75.1	64,399	75.5
Meru	101,971	63.6	104,890	65.9
Nandi	40,707	68.4	42,234	1.2
South Nyanza	106,810	73.8	103,178	3.2
Trans-Nzoia	35,668	65.9	36,492	7.2

Table 3.2 **Primary School Participation Rates by Gender and District* (cont'd)**

D. Female literacy
50-59%

Baringo	31,660	64.4	31,453	65.3
Busia	35,302	64.8	34,575	63.6
Kitui	55,454	61.6	56,551	63.8
Lamu	4,686	65.0	4,411	63.0
Siaya	60,244	69.1	59,239	69.5

E. Female literacy
less than 50%

Garissa	4,895	26.2	2,662	15.8
Isiolo	4,361	47.8	3,607	41.8
Kajiado	17,019	51.7	14,197	45.9
Kilifi	43,602	55.7	35,080	45.9
Kwale	27,391	54.1	22,689	45.6
Mandera	4,412	24.8	2,090	13.4
Marsabit	6,032	35.6	4,199	26.7
Narok	26,629	47.9	26,827	50.5
Samburu	4,524	31.7	3,129	22.8
Tana River	8,598	47.5	7,199	41.9
Turkana	5,411	22.4	3,840	16.8
Wajir	3,742	20.2	1,999	12.2
West Pokot	11,981	41.5	10,170	36.4
National	1,904,392	66.8	1,898,681	67.2

*Figures show primary school enrolment for 6-14 year olds instead of 6-13 year olds who should be in primary school. The resulting distortion is minor since only a few 14 year olds are in primary school.
**P.R is Participation Rate, which is the percentage of the age cohort 6-14 years in the population actually enrolled in primary school.

Source: Kenya Population Census, 1989, Volume 1, Table. 4.

Specifically, the provincial distribution of the districts with low primary schools participation is as follows:

Table 3.3 Districts Most Affected by Wastage

Coast Province	Eastern
Kilifi	Isiolo
Kwale	Marsabit
Tana River	Rift Valley
North-Eastern	Kajiado
Garissa	Narok
Mandera	Samburu
Wajir	Turkana
	West Pokot

Thus, conventional wisdom about low participation in schooling by children in pastoralist communities is supported by the kind of empirical evidence presented in the preceding paragraphs. It is significant to mention in this respect that surveyed Ministry of Education headquarters staff, who are the people involved in educational policy formulation in Kenya, accurately observed that wastage, particularly in the form of non-enrolment and dropout, is a major problem among pastoralist children (SPRED, 1994). This is a further reinforcement of the evidence that a discussion of problems of wastage in education, specifically at the primary level, in Kenya must incorporate children from pastoralist communities.

The third, and last, issue that the evidence presented in Table 3.2 and Table 3.3, allows us to resolve, relates to religion. Eight of the thirteen districts with low participation rates at the primary school level are also those regions in Kenya where Islam is the dominant religion. These are the three districts in Coast Province and North-Eastern Province, respectively and the two districts from Eastern Province.

In fact, the only other district where Islam is the majority religion that does not appear in Table 3.3 is Mombassa in Coast Province. The relatively favorable position of Mombassa in primary school participation results largely from two factors. First, the large non-Muslim population mainly from Kenya's hinterland that has over the years lived and/or settled in this dominantly metropolitan district. Mombassa is Kenya's second most populous city, with a 1989 population slightly over 460,000 (Government of Kenya, 1989). Second, the Muslim communities that live or work in

Mombassa have been more positively influenced than Muslims elsewhere by non-Muslim groups in Mombassa to enroll and attend school.

Again, senior Ministry of Education officials that were surveyed in our study in 1994, identified children in Islamic communities to be among groups most adversely affected by educational wastage at the primary school level (SPRED, 1994). As the evidence provided so far shows, this view of the senior staff of the Ministry of Education rests on solid foundation. In the Kenyan context, therefore, children of Muslim families are at great risk of failing to attend, and dropping out of, primary education.

In the literature reviewed regarding educational wastage in Kenya, poverty features prominently as a causal factor. Children of parents who lack the means to pay for various costs associated with schooling were reported to experience all the three components of educational wastage, but in particular non-enrolment and dropout (Eshiwani, 1984; Achola and Shiundu, 1991; Wamahiu, 1992). Poor parents also experience indirect costs because time children spend in school is an alternative to their labor and hence their contribution to family income (Briggs, 1973; Michieka, 1983;Verhine and Pita de Melo, 1988; Wamahiu, 1992).

In Kenya, many of the poor are to be found in rural communities and urban slums. In rural areas, many families are peasant farmers whose subsistence activities hardly generate sufficient income to meet many of their basic needs. In urban areas, the poor slum residents are usually involved in informal sector economic activities, which accrue very little income. In fact, in the major urban centers of Kenya, namely Nairobi, Mombassa and Kisumu, UNICEF supports educational programs for slum children in an attempt to improve their participation in primary school education (Shiundu and Achola, 1994).

Awareness that children of poor parents experience frequent incidents of non-enrolment, dropout and, to some extent, repetition, is widespread among those Kenyans who work in the educational sector. For instance, in the Strengthening Primary Education (SPRED) study conducted by the Bureau of Educational Research (BER) for the Ministry of Education (MoE), virtually all those cadre of the Ministry of Education personnel who were interviewed identified poverty as a leading cause of educational wastage (SPRED, 1994). In light of this and all the other evidence cited in the foregoing paragraphs, it is clear that children of the poor are among those sectors of Kenyan society among which educational wastage is an acute problem.

Faced with enormous difficulties in the provision of education for normal children, many African governments have historically paid very little attention to the education of the physically challenged children. Ignored to a large extent also has been early childhood education. In Kenya, the education of the physically challenged children and adults and of pre-school children (aged 3-6 years) has been left in the hands of communities, private groups and individuals, with funding coming mainly from donor agencies. Given that attendance of a pre-school education program is not mandatory for admission to primary school education, many children still have access to primary school education.

For the disabled children, there is the additional problem that their actual number in the Kenyan population is not known. The 1989 Population Census for the first time attempted to obtain information on the number of disabled persons; but any obtained figures grossly understated the number of persons with disabilities given a general pervasive reluctance in many households to report members with handicaps and, in a good number of cases, lack of awareness that certain behavioral characteristics constitute a handicap.

In the 1970s, the closest official position the Government of Kenya took regarding the education of the disabled was the establishment of the Kenya Institute of Special Education (KISE) to train teachers and other personnel for the affected children. Although in subsequent years the Government has made stronger pronouncements about its commitment to special education, public funds allocated to this sector of education have characteristically remained small. An examination of budgetary allocation to education involving this sector lends support to this observation. The provision of special education in Kenya remains the responsibility of donor agencies, communities and religious organizations. One serious difficulty is that donor support for this sector puts it at the mercy of political vicissitudes, which tend to characterize government-donor relations. On March 30, 1998 for instance, the Kenyan newspaper *Daily Nation* carried an urgent appeal to the Government to prevent special education from collapsing as major donors gave notice that they were withdrawing from funding this sector largely because some corrupt officers were diverting funds for personal benefit. Lack of substantial allocation of public funds to this sector means essentially that many of the disabled remain ill catered for by educational programs.

There is another category of children in Kenya, and elsewhere in Africa in any case, that has limited access to primary education. The umbrella term, which covers this group, is children in especially difficult circumstances (CEDC). This term is used to refer to, for example, street children, AIDS orphans, refugee children, children of prostitutes and children of imprisoned mothers (Okumu, 1992).

The problem of street children is an urban phenomenon; the number of such children has been rising rapidly in Kenya, especially since the implementation by the Government of World Bank and International Monetary Fund imposed structural adjustment policies (SAPS) in 1985. It is no coincidence that the number of street children, especially in the large urban centers of Nairobi, Mombassa and Kisumu, has been increasing between 1985 and 1996 when enrolment rates in primary school education declined steadily from 95 percent in 1985 to around 79 percent in 1996 (Government of Kenya Ministry of Education, 1997; UNESCO, 1998).

The problem of street children, especially in the capital city of Nairobi, has long been recognized and some organizations have responded to this situation. Organizations that have for long been involved in dealing with this problem are Undugu Society of Kenya, Action Aid Kenya, The Catholic Secretariat, and The National Council of Churches. Nonetheless, existing responses to this problem have been inadequate in the sense that only a small proportion of street children have been reached and rehabilitated. Since currently the numbers of street children are growing fast, the need to adequately address their basic educational needs is more urgent than ever before.

Similarly, another cadre of children in especially difficult circumstances, whose numbers are growing rapidly are HIV/AIDS orphans. The AIDS pandemic in Kenya is now both an urban and a rural phenomenon and Kenya currently ranks among the leading Eastern and Southern African countries in terms of incidences of AIDS infections. In the popular discourse on AIDS, Kenya is lumped together with Rwanda, Uganda and Zaire as Africa's AIDS belt. Indeed, there is now a conventional view that aids orphans will reach an alarming level by the start of the 21st century. Children orphaned by AIDS will require special support if they are to receive primary education.

In conclusion, a number of groups have been identified as particularly susceptible to the problem of wastage in primary school education. The groups may not be necessarily comprehensive, but in the Kenyan context they are the most salient. Individual children may belong simultaneously to two or more of these groups specified. The high risk groups in terms of wastage in primary education are as follows: girl children; most children from arid and semi-arid districts (children of pastoralists); most children of Islamic parents; children of poor rural parents and parents in urban slums; disabled children;

children in especially difficult circumstances; and mainly street children and AIDS orphans.

In the next chapter, we discuss the design of the research project on identifying the major factors which account for widespread educational wastage among children that belong to any one or a combination of the above groups. The factors are those identified by various categories of Ministry of Education staff, all of them heavily involved with the delivery of educational services to Kenyan children and youth.

4 A Design for Investigating Wastage

A design for the study of wastage involves systematic approaches for investigating the three components of wastage: non-enrolment, repetition and dropout. Broadly, each of the component is examined in terms of three crucial aspects; the perceived causes, the perceived solutions, and assessments of current initiatives with respect to achieving reductions in the contributions of each of the three components to wastage.

In 1993, the Bureau of Educational Research (BER) at Kenyatta University was contracted to assist the Ministry of Education with research on causes of and possible remedies for wastage in primary school education in Kenya. Funding for the wider project known as Strengthening Primary Education (SPRED), of which research was only one component, came from the British Government and was administered and monitored in Kenya through two British institutions namely the Overseas Development Administration (ODA) and the Center for British Teacher (CBT). The SPRED project was part of the Government of Kenya's cooperation with bilateral donor to pursue educational targets endorsed at the World Conference on Education for All (WCEFA) held in Jomtien Thailand in March 1990 and at the New York summit on the Rights of the Child in September 1990.

The main Jomtien and New York educational targets, which were identical and to which Kenya subscribed, were the following: a) Completion of primary school education by 80 percent of children aged 14 years by the year 2000; b) Universal access to basic education programs by the year 2000; c) Reduction of adult illiteracy rate to half of its 1990 level, which for Kenya (in 1989) stood at 20 percent for males and 40 percent of females (Government of Kenya, 1992).

These objectives were very ambitious in the Kenyan context, given facts on the ground. For instance, educational statistics for the primary (elementary) school level revealed considerable regional variations in school enrolment (participation) rates. About the time Kenya was endorsing the

61

Jomtien and New York educational goals, it was known that twelve districts including Kenya's two largest metropolitan districts of Nairobi and Mombasa had primary school enrolment rates below 65 percent. Districts in the arid and semi-arid parts of the country were particularly worse off in this regard as evidenced by enrolment rates of 37 percent for Marsabit, 26 percent for Mandera, and 14 percent for Wajir (UNICEF/GoK, 1992).

Moreover, educational statistics in the early 1990s were indicating further decline in enrolments in the country, implying that the worse off districts were most likely declining further and that other districts were joining the poor league.

Apart from this marked rate of non-enrolment in primary education, grade repetition in Kenyan primary schools is quite common. Because grade repetition is regarded as illegal, reliable figures on repeaters are difficult to come by. An official school census conducted in 1993 gave a national primary school repetition rate of about 11.6 percent (Republic of Kenya, 1994). This figure underestimates the magnitude of this problem and says nothing about the marked district variations (Ministry of Education, 1995).

Perhaps the gravest problem that was sure to obfuscate the Jomtien and New York goals was the rate of dropout in primary education in the country. The evidence has been overwhelming that on a national scale, only a little over 40 percent of any grade 1 cohort completes the full primary education cycle of 7 or 8 years depending on one's time frame (Achola, 1991a, and 1991b; Gichia, 1992; Wamahiu, 1992). This low primary school completion rate was also found to be the prevailing situation in UNICEF - supported districts of Baringo, Embu, Kisumu, Kitui, Kwale, Mombassa and South Nyanza (UNICEF/GoK, 1992: 97).

It was in light of the non-enrolment, repetition and dropout problems mentioned above and the need to find ways of meeting the Jomtien/New York educational goals that the Kenya Government entered into protracted negotiations with the British Government that resulted in the launching of the Strengthening of Primary Education (SPRED) Project in 1993.

The Scope of the SPRED Project

The project embraced three broad activities. The first involved strengthening the Planning Unit of the Ministry of Education particularly in the area of the collection, analysis and reporting of educational statistics. To this end, the Unit was to be computerized and its staff trained in data collection, management and analysis. The bulk of the data collected and analyzed was to shed light on trends in wastage in primary school education in the country's districts.

The second activity under SPRED was to expand and equip Teachers' Advisory Centers (TACs). New TACs were to be built in areas which had no access to them and these as well as the existing ones were to receive learning materials particularly in science subjects, mathematics and languages (English and Kiswahili). Tutors who managed these TACs were to receive additional training in the teaching of the mentioned subjects.

The third component of SPRED was an operational research project on wastage in primary education. The SPRED research project had two main phases. Phase 1 was devoted to illuminating factors which account for widespread lack of access to primary education (non-enrolment), frequent grade repetition by a large number of pupils (repetition), marked enrolment loss among pupils who join the primary school cycle (dropout). These three processes were encapsuled under the rubric, 'wastage', and were as already pointed out, the focus of Phase 1 of the SPRED research.

The phase 2 of the operational research on Strengthening Primary Education in Kenya was devoted to identifying and evaluating a number of initiatives or projects that were already attempting to increase access to primary education and or were trying to reduce both grade repetition and dropout from primary schools. In other words, phase 1 of the SPRED operational research was meant to reveal the magnitude of non-enrolment, grade repetition and dropout from primary education, the factors which account for these three aspects of educational wastage and remedial measures regarded as viable by various Ministry of Education cadre. Phase 2 went a little further in focusing on an assessment of intervention measures already in place to ameliorate various dimensions of educational wastage. It seems to us sound to outline the full mandate of the SPRED operational research project. The specific requirements for the team during this second phase were: a) To evaluate existing innovation and experimentation already present within the primary school system designed to address the problems of non-enrolment, repetition and dropout (wastage); b) To evaluate both local innovation and aid-assisted experiments; c) To evaluate the impact of the innovations, experimentation, both local and aid-assisted, on access to primary education and students' performance; d) To provide information on the relative cost of the impact achieved by each innovation/experiment; e) To identify those practices (innovations and experiments) which should be promoted and expanded in scale. In the cases of others, those factors which have caused the failure or lack of impact of the intervention; f) To assess the effectiveness of different means of targeting assistance to selected disadvantaged areas, schools and households where access is likely to be poorest.

It will readily be appreciated that a careful identification of the types of innovations or experiments that were considered to influence access to schooling, to promote efficient matriculation and retention in the primary school system was necessary. The impact of the selected innovations, their relative cost-effectiveness and their expansion and replication elsewhere in the country hinged on the accuracy with which relevant innovations were selected. This chapter accordingly focuses on a discussion of the rationale for the identification of the types of innovations to study and actual procedures through which individual projects were selected for in-depth evaluation.

Types of Innovations Identified for Study

Sometime in the early months of 1991, a consultant hired by the British Overseas Development Administration (ODA) held several consultative meetings with senior officers in the Ministry of Education in Nairobi and two senior scholars in the Bureau of Educational Research, Kenyatta University. It was mainly from these kinds of deliberations that the consultant identified some programs and projects that were being implemented to improve participation and retention of children in primary schooling in Kenya. These initiatives were subsequently outlined in the Terms of Reference document for use by investigators, in the following format. External aid interventions to include: a) World food program (WFP)-supported feeding program; b) Alternative curricula schools developed by UNDUGU Society; c) Assessment and placement of disabled school age children developed by the Danish International Development Agency (DANIDA); d) Support given to schools by major Non-Governmental Organizations (NGOs) such Action Aid and Plan International; e) Health and Community mobilization intervention by United Nations Children Fund (UNICEF).

In the case of local community – based innovations, those to be targeted should include: a) Various funding arrangements for books, teaching materials and buildings; b) Provision of extra tuition and teachers; c) Informal boarding arrangements; d) Child care arrangements that affect children's access to schools.

Once the research team and the Planning and Research Advisor (PRA) and the Research Methodology Consultant (RMC) were ready to start Phase 2, it became necessary to re-examine the kinds of innovations and experiments initially proposed in the Terms of Reference Document. It was the view of those involved in the discussion that the proposals in terms of Reference needed to be made more specific to subsequently facilitate easy identification of specific projects for evaluation. On the basis of several intensive meetings among those responsible for the SPRED operational research, the framework for evaluation which dichotomized innovations in terms of external aid assisted and local community based was retained; but the innovations were refined into distinct types and then the possible projects under each type were specified.

Based on the knowledge members of the research team had gained from the extensive review of literature on wastage in education in Kenya in phase 1 Part 1 of the SPRED research, and on the proposed solutions to wastage from the Ministry of Education Staff in Phase 1 part 2 of the SPRED study, an informal decision was made about the kinds of innovations that most effectively focused on educational wastage.

The final selection of the project for evaluation was made after extended discussion among members of the research team on the one hand and between the research team and the Planning and Research Advisor (PRA), and the Research Methodology Consultant (RMC) on the other hand. The last two persons represented the interest of the donor institution. It was accepted during these deliberations that, without necessarily distorting the spirit of the Terms of Reference, the initiatives to be evaluated would have to be those that addressed critical needs of children and served a large number of disadvantaged youth, especially girls, provided alternative educational programs for some of the children, and stood a good chance of being sustained for long time periods in the communities whose children were being served.

The refined outcome was the identification of four major initiative types or themes and some of the project activities under each theme. These are as follows.

Type 1. Health and Nutrition
- Community supported school feeding arrangements.
- Health and community mobilization interventions by UNICEF.

Type 2. Non - Formal Education
- Alternative curricula schools developed by UNDUGU.

- Innovations/experimentations focusing on 'out of school' children, including street children.
- Innovations/experimentations related to assisting pregnant girls and curbing early (child) marriages.
- Initiatives by other NGOs, e.g. Action Aid and Plan International.

Type 3. School Facilities and Resources
- Various funding arrangements for books, teaching materials and buildings.
- Informal boarding arrangements.
- Support given to schools by major NGO's such as Action Aid and Plan International.

Type 4. Community Initiatives
- Provision of extra tuition and teachers.
- Rearrangements of time-tables in response to local conditions.
- Initiatives to integrate religious education and mainstream schooling by some Muslim community groups developed in Coast and North-Eastern provinces.
- Initiatives to increase community awareness of the value of education and the problems of wastage.

It is appropriate to add here that after completion of field work, and careful reflection, two projects among those that were evaluated, did not comfortably fit in any of the four types shown in the box. These two seemed to share characteristics, which called for classification into an independent category. As a result, a fifth initiative type was identified and labeled as Integrated Initiatives.

Identification of Specific Projects

Most of the projects reported in this chapter were identified prior to the start of fieldwork. Some had been specified, even if somewhat broadly, in Terms of Reference Document. Others were identified from the information provided by senior officers in the Ministry of Education, senior scholars in the research team under the ambit of the Bureau of Educational Research at Kenyatta University and officers of other initiatives in headquarter offices in Nairobi.

There were, however, a few projects among those subsequently evaluated that were identified during field work in a number of districts.

These initiatives were regarded as directly relevant to the reduction of educational wastage and therefore merited inclusion in the evaluation strategy.

Eight of the projects (32%) focused on non-formal education initiatives; 6 projects (24%) were concerned with the provision of school facilities and resources; another 6 were community initiatives; projects targeting health and nutrition programs were 3; and only 2 projects were multipurpose integrated initiatives. The two integrated projects were the direct initiatives of communities and included Mukuru Promotion Center and Kabiro Community Center, all in the city of Nairobi.

The evaluated projects were drawn from 10 districts, which included Baringo, Embu, Kiambu, Kisume, Kwale, Mombassa, Nairobi, Nyeri, Samburu and Tuokona. These districts were identified largely on account of their severe educational wastage rates based on the 1989 population census which provided information on children aged 6 to 14 years who had 'left school' or had ' never attended school'; and the 1993 primary school census data on proportion of repeaters and dropouts and pupil enrolment rates as well as proportions of 'trained' and 'untrained' teachers.

In terms of geographical location within Kenya, the selected districts are from arid and semi-arid parts of the Rift valley, Eastern and North Eastern provinces, from the largely Islamic Coast province and the three large urban centers of Nairobi, Mombassa and Kisumu. The only exceptions to the criteria used were Kiamba and Nyeri whose inclusion was based on the fact that they had community- supported school feeding programs.

Table 4.1   A List of Projects Evaluated and Fully Reported (Type of Initiative)

Project name	Sites	Location
UNICEF, Bamako (1)	Several sites in rural areas	Baringo
UNICEF, Bamako (1)	10 sites in urban areas, 50 sites in rural areas	Kisumu
National School Feeding Council of Kenya (1)	A number of schools in the two districts	Kiambu and Nyeri
Action Aid (2)	Karibongi Slums	Nairobi
Compassion International (2)	Gachoka Division	Embu
Plan International (2)	Gachoka and Siakiago Divisions	Embu
Christian Children's Fund (2)	Baragoi Maralal Nyiro and Wamba Divisions	Samburu
Wamba World Vision Project (2)	Wamba Division	Samburu
Stephan Kanja Primary School (2)	Majimboni Simba Hills	Kwale
Undugu Basic Education Program (3)	Kariobangi, Kibera, Mathare and Pumwani Divisions	Nairobi
Jamma Home (3)	Uhuru Estate	Nairobi
Kisumu Evening Continuation Classes(3)	Arina, Kaloleni, Kisumu Union and Kisumu Central Centers, Urban Kamadhira and Awasi Holo Centers (rural)	
Nadrikonyen Catholic Street Children (3)	Lodwar Town	Turkana
Pandperi Street Children Program (3)	Kisumu Municipality	Kisumu
Bendera Baragoi Out of School Program (3)	Baragoi Town	Samburu
Wema Center (3)	Likoni Division	Mombassa
St. John's (3)	Pumwani Community Slums	Nairobi
Madrasa Resource Center (4)	14 centers in Mombassa Town	Mombassa

Table 4.1   **A List of Projects Evaluated and Fully Reported (Type of Initiative) (cont'd)**

Islamic Al-Noor Nursery School (Jamia Mosque) (4)	Lodwar Town	Turkana
Muhaka Islamic Center (4)	Diani Zone	Kwale
Inuka Self Help (4)	Likoni Primary and Nursery School	Mombassa
Waa Primary School (4)	Ngombeni/Waa Kwale	Kwale
Kongowea Community School (4)	Kingeleni Zone	Mombassa
Mukuru Promotion Center (4)	Nairobi South B	Nairobi
Kabiro Community Slums Center (4)	Kawangware	Nairobi

(1) Health and Nutrition; (2) School Facilities and Resources; (3) Non-formal Education; (4) Community.

Selection of Informants

Individuals who provided information in this study consisted of persons who had direct links with the different projects sampled for evaluation. There were several categories of such informants. The first category included owners or proprietors of the initiatives identified for evaluation. The second group were those responsible for the management of the initiatives and included project directors and officers. The third category of informants were those with the supervisory roles in the projects and included committee chairpersons, head teachers, teachers, social workers, and others of equivalent rank. The fourth and last group of informants were drawn from the intended beneficiaries of the various projects; they were mainly primary school pupils, other children of comparable age and parents of both types of children.

Since owners or proprietors of the initiatives studied were rarely at project sites, being mainly available in the headquarters offices in Nairobi, only a few of them were interviewed. As a result, more project directors and senior project officers in the field stations were the ones interviewed for detailed information on specific projects.

In addition, personnel at the level of supervisors and administrative cadre just below the supervisory level were also interviewed, as were primary school children and other children of equivalent age brackets and some of their parents. The common denominator was that those sampled for detailed interviews were expected to be fully knowledgeable about the various projects and so even when there were only informants, useful information about projects was still obtained.

It is not surprising that administrative roles from which were samples drawn, more men than women were part of the sample. As a result, more men than women were interviewed. Among the students (pupils) there was a better balance between the sample of girls and boys, which is also a more accurate reflection of the proportion of girls and boys in schools at this level of education. The over- representation of men in the non-pupil samples is also a reflection of men's over-representation in the various supervisory and administrative roles in the projects that were surveyed.

Information Gathering Tools

In evaluation research, one needs to know the purpose or aims for which certain programs or projects were started, and how the organizational arrangements and activities put in place promote and/or hinder the attainment of the intended aims. A lot more information may be collected about the programs or projects but the ultimate focus of any evaluation research remains the efficiency with which the objectives are being attained. In reference to the evaluation study a wide range of questions were included in the interview instruments for collecting required information.

The whole thrust of the fieldwork was to conduct in-depth interviews on: a) background information about projects; b) project objectives, activities and their implementation; c) what the projects provide to intended beneficiaries; d) the impact of the projects on the beneficiaries in particular and their community in general. The interviewing of beneficiaries focused heavily on the impact of the project on them.

Two interview schedules were used, one for non-pupil informants and the other, albeit a brief one, for pupil informants and other youth of equivalent age that were served by some of the projects. The non-pupil interview schedule was subdivided into three main sections. Section A merely solicited for such background information as the name of the sponsors of the projects, the date it was started, its physical location and the geographical scope of its operations. Section B asked for the stated aims of the projects and the organizational arrangements and the activities that were being implemented towards the pursuit of the projects objectives. Section C went into the great details about the activities of each project classified by type of initiative. In other words, specific but similar questions covered projects classified under Health and Nutrition initiatives; and specific though shared information focused on projects under School Facilities and Resources. Similar procedure was used for projects classified under Community Initiative and Integrated Initiatives.

Section D had common questions about impact of the various projects irrespective of type. Included in this section were questions about problems experienced in implementation, measures, plans, if any, to sustain some externally sponsored projects once such sponsorship terminates.

The pupil interview schedule asked whether or not pupils were aware of the objectives of the project serving them, what they liked about the project, what impact the project had on their lives and work, what ideas they had for making the project work better.

Administration of Interviews

Responsibility for data collection was divided among members of the research team. Senior researcher accompanied by a senior Ministry of Education Officer and two or more trained research assistants were responsible for evaluation of projects in two districts of the ten districts covered by the entire study.

Two strategies were followed during data collection. Data were collected by means of individual interviews and focus-group interviews. Many of the project managers and supervisors were interviewed individually; others were interviewed in groups as part of a group. All the student beneficiaries were subjected to focus-group interviews. Both in the case of individual and group interviews, two members of the research team co-operated in the interviewing process; one member posed the questions to the informants and the other member wrote down the responses. This strategy proved to be quick and allowed for recording of more accurate responses than would be obtained by having one researcher perform both tasks.

In the majority of cases, key members of the research team asked questions while the research assistants did the recording of the responses.

Occasionally, the two reversed their roles without any bad effect on the research process.

It was widely reported by members of the research teams that many of the informants were co-operative and readily and honestly responded to the questions when they clearly understood them. The only real difficulty was experienced with questions to project managers and supervisors regarding funds spent on various aspects of the project. Usually the response was that they did not know or had no authority from senior officers at headquarters offices to disclose such information. In a number of instances, the informants deliberately declined to provide this information.

5 Extent and Perceived Causes of Wastage

This chapter examines the extent of the various components of wastage and their perceived causes in the Kenyan context. The problem of wastage is pervasive in Africa. The extent of wastage in Kenya is representative of wastage problem in the African region. This assumption is tested by examining the characteristics of the distributions of African countries on the extent of non-enrolment, and repetition.

Standardization of the distributions of non-enrolment and repetition provides an effective approach to make inter-country comparisons. Three distributions are examined; male non-enrolment rates, female non-enrolment rates, and female repetition rates. Data on male repetition rates for African Countries were not available. The UN data sources provided, aggregate male and female repetition rates (UNESCO Statistical Year Book, 1990). Separate figures for female repetition are available but not for males. Countries are grouped into three categories. Those countries, which had standardized scores, below −1.00 standard deviation on non-enrolment ratios, are grouped in the high non-enrolment category. Countries, which have standardized scores, above 1.00 standard deviation on non-enrolment ratio, are in low non-enrolment category. The rest are in the middle category. Countries, which had standardized scores below −1.00 standard deviation, on repetition rates, are grouped in the low repetition category. African nations, which have standardized scores above 1.00 standard deviation, on repetition rates, are in high repetition category. The remaining nations are in middle category.

Table 5.1 presents the classification of African countries on the two dimensions of wastage, non-enrolment and repetition. There are three countries with low female non-enrolment rates. They are Namibia, Swaziland and Togo. When male non-enrolments are considered Congo, Malawi and Tunisia join the category of low non-enrolment countries. The countries with high non-enrolment rates for either males or females are Burkina Faso, Djibouti, Ethiopia, Mali and Niger.

Table 5.1 Classification of African Countries on Rates of Male-Female Non-Enrolment and Female Repetition

Category Type	Female Non-enrolment	Male Non-enrolment	Female Repetition
A. Low	Namibia Swaziland Togo	Congo, Malawi, Namibia, Swaziland, Togo, Tunisia	Botswana, Egypt, Tanzania, Zambia
B. Middle	Algeria Benin Botswana Cape Verde Chad Comoros Congo Cote D' Egypt E. Guinea Eritrea Gambia Guinea Kenya Lesotho Malawi Mauritania Mauritius Morocco Mozambique S. Africa Tunisia Tanzania Zaire Zambia	Algeria Benin Botswana Cape Verde Chad Comoros Cote D' Egypt E. Guinea Eritrea Gambia Guinea Kenya Lesotho Mauritania Mauritius Morocco Mozambique S. Africa Tanzania Zaire Zambia	Algeria Benin Burkina F Cape Verde Cote D' Djibouti E. Guinea Eritrea Ethiopia Gambia Guinea Swaziland Tunisia Kenya Lesotho Malawi Mali Mauritania Mauritius Morocco Mozambique Namibia S. Africa Zaire

**Table 5.1 Classification of African Countries on Rates of Male-
Female Non-Enrolment and Female Repetition (cont'd)**

C. High	Burkina Faso	Burkina Faso	Chad
	Djibouti	Djibouti	Comoros
	Ethiopia	Ethiopia	Congo
	Mali	Mali	Togo
	Niger	Niger	
Total	N=33	N=33	N=33

Source: UNICEF Statistical Year Books, 1990.

The African countries with high female repetition rates are a different group of countries than those with high female non-enrolment rates. This is to be expected, as factors which lead to high non-enrolment rates, are often dissimilar to those which influence the process of repetition in schools. The countries with low female repetition rates are Botswana, Egypt, Tanzania and Zambia.

Kenya is among some 70 per cent of African countries which fall in the middle category with respect to non-enrolment and repetition. Having located Kenya relative to other African countries in reference to wastage, we now examine the problem of wastage in the ten Kenyan districts that were targeted for study. The 1989 Kenya Census provides data on two components of wastage, dropout and non-enrolment. The data on repetition are estimates and are from a primary school survey conducted by the Ministry of Education in 1993. The data on dropout and non-enrolment are limited to population aged 10-14 years of age. Nevertheless, these data indicate the extent of primary school dropout and non-enrolment problem in the 10-study district. The data for dropout and non-enrolment rates are presented in Table 5.2.

Table 5.2 Non-Enrolment and Dropout Rates in the Ten Districts

District	Non-Enrolment*		Dropout	
	Male	Female	Male	Female
Baringo	15.9	16.3	2.3	2.5
Kajiado	35.2	43.0	5.5	6.4
Kakamega	11.0	12.0	4.2	4.3
Kisumu	6.3	9.1	3.3	5.5
Kitui	10.5	10.6	3.3	3.3
Kwale	25.4	39.5	6.0	8.4
Meru	14.2	12.8	5.6	4.8
Mombassa	11.9	28.6	7.2	15.8
Nairobi	25.8	25.9	7.7	13.2
Nyandarua	6.6	6.5	3.8	3.8

Dropout rate is the number of students who discontinue schooling in a given year out of 100 students who initially enrolled at the beginning of the school year. Non-enrolment rate is the number of children who failed to attend school out of 100 children aged 10-14 years. Repetition is a form or retention. The number of students in a given year in the school who are retained in the same grade are counted as repeaters. Repetition is the number of students out of 100 in a previous grade that is retained in the same grade. In all the districts, except Meru the female dropout rates were slightly higher. The district of Meru had a higher male dropout rate. The district of Meru has a strong plantation economy with a large demand for child labor. The two large Kenyan cities, Nairobi and Mombassa, have exceptionally high dropout rates. In particular, female dropout rates in Nairobi and Mombassa are almost twice as high as male dropout rates. Both Nairobi and Mombassa are large cities.

The national non-enrolment rate for males was 12.6 and for females 14.5. Non-enrolment rates were considerably higher than the dropout rates in all the 10 districts. Four districts, Baringo, Kajiado, Kwale and Nairobi had male non-enrolment rates much above the national rate. The same four districts also had female non-enrolment rates beyond the national female rate. A fifth district, Mombassa had a female non-enrolment rate about twice the national female non-enrolment rate. The gap between female and male non-enrolments rates was the highest in Mombassa. In this district, the female non-enrolment rate was about 2.5 times as high as the male non-enrolment rate. The estimated repetition rates in the 10 study districts are presented in Table 5.3.

Table 5.3 Repetition Rates by Sex in the Ten Districts (%)

District	Boys		Girls		Total	
	N	%	N	%	N	%
Baringo	7,035	8.4	7,008	8.3	14,043	16.7
Kajiado	2,364	6.1	1,792	4.7	4,156	10.8
Kakamega	13,638	5.1	13,145	4.9	26,783	10.0
Kisumu	11,677	7.5	10,670	6.8	22,347	14.3
Kitui	10,205	5.9	9,766	5.6	19,971	11.5
Kwale	2,166	2.8	1,672	2.2	3,838	5.0
Meru	11,098	5.3	10,951	5.2	22,049	10.4
Mombassa	808	1.4	639	1.0	1,447	2.4
Nairobi	2,209	1.8	1,800	1.5	4,009	3.3
Nyandarua	3,830	3.5	3,521	3.2	7,351	6.7
Kenya		6.0		5.6		11.6

Source: 1993 Primary School Census Data, Ministry of Education, Nairobi.

The national repetition rate for 1993 was 6.0 percent for boys and 5.6 percent for girls. (See Table 5.3). The districts with higher than national repetition rate were Baringo and Kisumu. This was true for males and females. Baringo had a high non-enrolment rate. Kisumu district, which was not among districts with either high non-enrolment or dropout rates, experienced high repetition rate in 1993.

The objective data clearly suggests high rates of non-enrolment, repetition and dropout. The intensity of each of the three components of wastage varies across districts. We found that Mombassa had the highest dropout rate among females; Kajiado had the highest rate of non-enrolment for both girls and boys. Baringo district has the highest repetition rate.

It was in light of the non-enrolment, repetition and dropout problems and the need to find ways of meeting the Jomtien/New York educational goals that the Kenya Government entered into protracted negotiations with the British Government that resulted in the launching of the Strengthening of Primary Education (SPRED) Project in 1993.

As mentioned in Chapter 4, three processes were encapsulated under the rubric, 'wastage', and were as already pointed out, the focus of Phase 1 of the SPRED research.

The study investigated the perceived magnitude of non-enrolment, repetition and dropout. Data on teachers and head teacher's perceptions of the magnitude of each of the three components of wastage are presented in Table 5.4. The proportions of teachers and head teachers who reported non-enrolment, as the most critical wastage problem was the largest in Kajiado District. Furthermore, the proportions of teachers and head teachers who reported repetition as the most critical wastage problem was highest in Baringo District. Among teachers and head teachers who were surveyed, Kwale had the largest proportion that reported dropout. These data closely support the trends revealed by census data.

One of the objectives of the survey was to investigate the perceived causes of each of the three aspects of wastage. The focus was on the extent of variation of the perceived causes across educational personnel in the ten districts. The investigation of variations across educational staff and districts has important implication for educational policy formulation in Kenya.

The perceived causes were identified from stated opinions of the survey respondents. The sources of opinion are three categories of educational staff, teacher, head teacher and local educational leaders. These three categories are the immediate providers of education. The extent and intensity of perceived barriers to provision of education many vary among the three providers. The focus of methodology was to elicit as many opinions about the causes of wastage among the three categories of educational staff. Therefore each one interviewed expressed an array of opinions in terms of the causes of wastage. The number of responses varies across respondents. It should be noted that the questions were open ended. The respondents as mentioned earlier came from the 10 districts.

Table 5.4 Teachers' and Head Teachers' Perceptions of Extent of the Three Components of Wastage (%)*

	Teachers			Head-teachers		
District	Non-Enrolment >10%	Repetition >10%	Drop-out >10%	Non-Enrolment >10%	Repetition >10%	Drop-out >10%
Baringo	36.7	67.8	35.0	18.2	63.7	22.7
	(180)	(180)	(180)	(22)	(22)	(22)
Kajiado	68.9	62.9	45.7	66.7	60.0	20.0
	(103)	(103)	(103)	(15)	(15)	(15)
Kakamega	37.3	54.9	31.7	50.0	27.8	11.2
	(153)	(153)	(153)	(18)	(18)	(18)
Kisumu	33.0	50.4	38.9	25.0	31.3	18.8
	(113)	(113)	(113)	(16)	(16)	(16)
Kitui	54.0	51.1	61.5	42.8	42.9	28.6
	(135)	(135)	(135)	(21)	(21)	(21)
Kwale	54.4	78.7	69.9	46.6	20.0	33.3
	(136)	(136)	(136)	(15)	(15)	(15)
Meru	26.4	45.0	44.3	8.0	25.0	0.0
	(231)	(231)	(231)	(8)	(8)	(8)
Mombassa	59.4	48.9	49.0	37.5	25.0	0.0
	(96)	(96)	(96)	(8)	(8)	(8)
Nairobi	30.0	44.0	46.5	33.3	6.7	6.7
	(191)	(191)	(191)	(15)	(15)	(15)
Nyandarua	6.4	12.1	19.3	0.0	5.9	5.9
	(157)	(157)	(157)	(17)	(17)	(17)

*Figures in parentheses are actual sample sizes.

The universe of opinions contained a variety of causes related to the three aspects of educational wastage. An analytical approach was developed to identify causes, which were frequently identified by the informants. The analytical approach was as follows: a) The causes mentioned by each category of educational staff were separately identified across the ten districts; b) These causes were then counted and the frequency of causes mentioned was obtained; c) The frequencies of a few causes were very low. These causes, which were less than ten percent of the universe of mentions, were dropped; d) The remaining causes were ranked in descending order on the basis of frequencies of mentions; e) The causes that received the first, second and third ranks were identified; f) These three ranks were separately obtained for each of the three categories of educational staff; g) The frequencies with which each of these ranked causes occurred across the ten districts were tabulated; h) These tabulations yielded the modes for each of the causes ranked one through three; i) This approach was repeated for each of the three categories of informants namely, teachers, head teachers and local educational leaders.

Table 5.5 presents all the causes of non-enrolment mentioned by teachers, head teachers and local. There were eight causes, which were mentioned by more than ten percent of the members in any one of the three categories consisting of teachers, head teachers and local education leaders.

Table 5.5 Salient Causes of Non-Enrolment Listed Randomly

1: Parental ignorance including neglect of education for girls.
2: Involvement of children in wage labor employment.
3: Poverty among parents and community resulting in lack of money for School levies.
4: Presence of female specific risks such as pregnancy.
5: Harsh environmental conditions such as lack of water, food and long distances to schools.
6: Poor home climate, family problems, instability, child deviance.
7: Lack of pre-school places and pre-school exposure.
8: Lack of school places, few and poor learning facilities and resource.

An examination of Table 5.5 reveals a number of structural factors out side the schools' control. The conceptual framework presented in chapter 2 suggests that some of the mentioned causes of non-enrolment may be the result of independent as well as interactive effects of community participation, in education, school staff activities and availability of resources.

Table 5.6 presents data in terms of the three most important causes of non-enrolment as rated by teachers, head teachers and local educational leaders. The rationale for focusing on three most important causes was to high light those causes, which may require the immediate urgent attention of policy makers. As mentioned earlier in this chapter, the three most important causes may vary across teachers, head teachers, and local educational leaders and across districts.

Table 5.6 Frequencies of Mentions of Ordered Causes of Non-Enrolment by Three Categories of Ministry of Education Staff

Category of staff	Ranking of causes		
	Most important	Second most important	Third most important
I: Teachers (N=1495)	Parental ignorance including neglect of girl's education	Parental ignorance including neglect of girl's education	Wage employment among children
No. of districts	6	3	3
II: Head Teachers	Parental ignorance including neglect of girl's education	Parental ignorance including neglect of girl's education	Parental/ Community poverty
No. of districts	6	4	6
III: Local Educational Leaders (N=268)	Parental/ Community poverty	Parental/ Community poverty	Wage employment among children
No. of districts	4	3	2

Among teachers from each of six districts, parental ignorance was identified as the most significant cause of non-enrolment. Teachers in additional three districts rated this cause as the second most important cause of non-enrolment. The third most important perceived cause of non-enrolment among teachers was wage employment among children. This cause was mentioned by teachers in only three of the ten districts. Thus, from the perspective of teachers, the most important (because most frequently mentioned) perceived cause of non-enrolment was parental ignorance.

In the case of head teacher's parental ignorance was again mentioned as the most important perceived cause of non-enrolment. Head teachers in six districts rated it as the leading cause of non-enrolment. Teachers from the remaining four districts rated this cause of non-enrolment as second in importance. According to the head teachers, the third most important cause of non-enrolment was parental/communal poverty. Teachers in six of the ten districts rated this cause as third in importance. These data suggest that according to head teachers, parental ignorance clearly ranks as the leading cause of non-enrolment across districts.

For local educational leaders, parental/communal poverty ranked as the leading cause of non-enrolment. In four of the ten districts, local educational leaders identified this cause as the most important. In additional three districts, parental/communal poverty was identified as the second most importance cause of non-enrolment. This cause however tied with parental ignorance as the second most salient cause of non-enrolment. More over local educational leaders in two districts rated two causes, wage employment among children, and long distance to school as the third most critical causes.

In sum, parental ignorance emerged as the most salient cause of non-enrolment. This is due to the high consensus among teachers and head teachers with regard to the leading causes of non-enrolment. There is also homogeneity among teachers and head teachers in ranking the salient causes across the ten districts. The local educational leaders differed from teachers and head teachers in their perceptions of the leading causes of non-enrolment. Among the local educational leaders there was considerable heterogeneity in terms of the causes of non-enrolment. This is indicated by a large number of causes mentioned by local educational leaders.

As we show next, the major reasons for non-enrolment are different from those for repetition. That is, while mainly factors within the community account for the former, in the case of the latter the factors are situated mainly within the school. Indeed, this is what the conceptual model had anticipated. We examine the causes of grade repetition as perceived by teachers, head teachers and local educational leaders in the next section.

Grade Repetition

A wide range of factors was mentioned by all the three types of educational personnel as causes of grade repetition. These perceived causes are shown in Table 5.7. Knowledge among the three categories of educational staff about the causes of grade repetition appears deeper than their knowledge of the causes of non-enrolment. Evidence of this is the greater variety of causes of repetition that were identified. This is to be expected since unlike non-enrolment, the activity of grade repetition is something that occurs within the school system in which these educational staff works.

Most causes of repetition are specific to practices that take place within the school system.

Table 5.7 Identified Salient Causes of Grade Repetition

1: Irregular school attendance due to child deviance, ill health transfers.

2: Inadequate learning facilities, resources, staffing.

3: Heavy emphasis on examinations, holding back children due to poor examination performance.

4: Enrolment of over-age or under-age children.

5: Environmental hardship, insecurity leading to irregular school attendance, poor learning.

6: Involvement by children in competing cultural practices and activities.

7: Lack of exposure to pre-school education.

8: Involvement by children in wage employment and child labor.

9: Bad effects of co-educational classes.

10: Holding children back by parents due to lack of funds.

11: Poor teaching and learning, lack of commitment to work by teachers, lack of interest by teachers and parents leading to poor academic performance.

12: Poor school administration, frequent teacher absenteeism.

Among twelve causes of grade repetition presented in Table 5.7 only three, namely environmental constraints, involvement by children in competing activities, and participation by children wage employment, are non-school factors. The remaining nine causes are directly linked to the school setting.

Table 5.8 shows the results of analysis in terms of the three most important causes of repetition that were identified by the three categories of Ministry of Education personnel. Teachers in seven out of the sampled ten districts rated irregular attendance of school by pupils as the leading cause of class or grade repetition. Teachers in three districts rated preoccupation of schools with good performance in the Kenya Certificate of Primary Education

(KCPE) examination taken at the end of the primary school cycle, as the second most important cause of class repetition. At the same time, teachers in three other districts rated this factor (preoccupation with schools performance in the KCPE examination), as the third most important cause of class repetition by pupils. Also receiving mention among teachers in three districts as the third most important cause of class repetition was involvement in wage employment by children who were already enrolled in school.

It is instructive that just as in the case of teachers, head teachers also ranked irregular attendance of school by pupils as the leading cause of class repetition. Teachers in six districts rated this factor as the leading contributor to class repetition. Apart from this factor, head teachers were divided on the second and third most important causes of repetition. Thus, both heavy focus of the school curriculum on the KCPE examination and inadequate teaching and learning resources in schools as contributors to class repetition tied for second place in three districts each. The third place went to an entirely new factor, lack of exposure to pre-school experience by children. The last factor was rated third by head teachers in four districts.

In the case of local educational administrators, poor school climate was identified as the leading cause of class repetition. The factor was rated as a leading cause in four of the eight districts where local educational administrators had been interviewed on this specific question. Among issues that constituted poor school climate were lack of commitment to work by teachers and pupils, poor teaching and learning, and poor performance in examinations by pupils. These factors constituted a syndrome that depressed the academic standards of pupils and in so doing compelled many of them to repeat a grade during matriculation through the primary school cycle.

Irregular attendance of school by pupils was identified by sampled local educational administrators as the second most important cause of class repetition by pupils. This response emerged from local educational administrators in three districts (see Table 5.8).

Table 5.8 also shows that local educational administrators in 3 districts rated inadequate teaching and learning materials in schools as the third most important cause of class repetition.

Table 5.8 Frequencies of Mentions of Ordered Causes of Repetition by Three Categories of Ministry of Education Staff

Categories of staff	Ranking of causes		
	Most important	Second most important	Third most important
I: Teachers (N=1495)	Irregular attendance of school	Emphasis on examinations	Emphasis on examination
No. of districts	7	3	3
Issues thus rated	N.A	N.A	Wage employment among children
II. Head Teachers (N=172)	Irregular attendance of school	Inadequate school resources	Lack of pre-school experience
No. of Districts	6	3	4
Issues thus rated	N.A	Emphasis on examinations	N.A
III. Local Educational Leaders (N=268)	Poor school climate	Irregular attendance of school	Inadequate school resources
No. of districts	4	3	3

N.A= Not applicable

The main conclusions to be drawn from Table 5.8 are, first, that irregular attendance of school by pupils emerged as the leading cause of class repetition. This is so because this factor received the most important rating among both teachers and head teachers in most of the districts studied, and also second most important ranking among local educational leaders. Second, undue preoccupation with performance by pupils, and ranking of schools on national examination appeared as the second most salient cause of class repetition. This factor was frequently mentioned by teachers and head teachers in a good number of the surveyed districts. Third, lack of adequate facilities and resources in schools to promote effective learning received two mentions, one each by head teachers and local educational administrators, thus making it the third most salient cause of class repetition. Such other causes of class repetition as wage employment among some pupils, poor school climate and lack of pre-school experience by some pupils, received only occasional mention.

The overriding conclusion, therefore, is that the salient causes of class repetition by pupils are school specific. In this respect, while their resolution may involve paying attention to some issues outside the schools, the main focus of such resolution must be on processes, which go on within the school system itself. In the next section, our attention shifts to what the three categories of educational personnel surveyed state as the causes of dropout from school by pupils.

Dropout from School

The causes of dropout from school that were frequently mentioned by the teachers, head teachers and local educational administrators are shown in Table 5.9. The seven salient causes of dropout mentioned are strikingly similar to those that were identified as responsible for non-enrolment in school by some children. The major departure this time around is that the causes affect children who are actually enrolled in school. The significance of this fact is that most of the reasons for dropping out of school emanate from factors both within the school system and within households or the larger community.

For instance, of the first four causes of dropout mentioned, three clearly arise from out of school and within school factors. These causes are parental or community poverty which forces some children to take up paid work as an alternative to schooling; lack of counseling and guidance services for parents as well as for pupils regarding the benefits of schooling, especially for girls; the latter then tend to be lured into risky sexual activity, often involving adult male members of the community; teenage pregnancy and for child marriages which terminate the education of girls.

Table 5.9 Important Causes of Dropout from Formal School

1: Parental/Community poverty resulting in child labor.
2: Irregular school attendance leading to poor performance and frequent class repetition.
3: Lack of Proper guidance for pupils and parents leading to neglect of education for girls and exposing them to sex related risks.
4: Teenage pregnancy and early (child) marriages especially among girls attending school.
5: Harsh environment, insecurity and long distances to school.
6: Negative peer influence, family instability leading to deviance among some pupils.
7: Enrolment of over-age children who fail to concentrate on schooling.

It should be noted, moreover, that the second mentioned cause of dropout namely irregular attendance of school by some pupils, which results in examination failure and hence class repetition and ultimately in quitting schooling altogether, is closely related to the sixth factor, bad peer influence as well as poor and unstable family environment. Irregular attendance of school is a form of pupil deviance and often results from negative peer values in and outside school and from unstable family relations. Both factors, therefore, operate within and outside the school to cause the attrition of some pupils from schooling.

The seventh and last factor mentioned as a cause of dropout namely enrolment of relatively older pupils, plays itself out in the school and outside in the community. In school, older children may fail to continue schooling where their younger peers make them feel (academically) inferior or when they themselves feel uncomfortable about sharing lessons with younger pupils. Outside the school, older pupils are more likely than their younger colleagues to engage in activities, which compete with schooling. Examples include being sexually active, attending social events such as dancing and cultural festivities such initiation ceremonies. Ultimately, such activities lead some of the older pupils to drop out from school.

Results in Table 5.10 draw attention to the three most important causes of dropout from school by pupils according to the views of the three categories of educational staff surveyed in Kenya. Teachers in seven out of the ten districts that were covered rated parental and/or community poverty that often leads to child labor, as the leading cause of dropout from school. These seven districts include areas of high agricultural potential or relatively easy access to urban amenities. Moreover, in six out of these seven districts, head teachers shared the views of the teachers that poverty was the leading cause of dropout from school by pupils. The lone district where the head teachers differ from the teachers' view, the former identified poor academic performance by pupils as the leading cause of dropout from school. In identifying this cause, the head teachers seem to have touched on an issue, which singled the district (Nyandarua) out as an area where good academic performance was over-emphasized and led pupils to quit school if they were diagnosed to be academically mediocre or very weak.

In the eight districts where local educational administrators/leaders were surveyed, rating leading cause of departure from schooling is evenly divided between poverty and teenage pregnancy. Thus, local educational administrators in four districts identified parental/community poverty as the leading contributor to dropout from school.

In the remaining four districts, these officers identified teenage pregnancy leading to early marriage as the leading cause of dropout from school. There is nothing peculiar to these four districts as they reflect both economically sound parts and economically poor parts of Kenya.

In view of the evidence cited above in reference to dropout from school, the leading cause of this aspect of educational wastage is parental-cum-community poverty. As Table 5.10 suggests, this factor receives first rating among both teachers and head teachers in 70 per cent of the surveyed districts and in 50 per cent of the districts in which local educational leaders rated the various causes of educational wastage.

There was much less consensus among the educational personnel surveyed on the second most important cause of dropout from school. Part of this lack of consensus is reflected in the relatively few districts in which the different categories of these educational staff shared perceptions about the second most important cause of dropout from school; and in ties in the mention of the second most important cause among the same category of staff in separate districts. In this connection, in no more than four districts did the educational personnel shown in Table 5.10 identify in a significant way the second most salient cause of dropout from school.

Table 5.10 Frequencies of Mentions of Ordered Causes of Dropout by Three Categories of Ministry of Education Staff

Categories of staff	Ranking of causes		
	Most important	Second most important	Third most important
Teachers (N=1495)	Parental/Community Poverty & child labor	Harsh, insecure environment	- Lack of proper guidance - Risks involved in educating girls
No. of districts	7	3	5
Issue thus rated	N.A	-Lack of proper Guidance -Risks involved in educating girls	N.A
No. of districts	-	3	-
Head teacher (N=172)	Parental/community Poverty & child labor	-Irregular school attendance -Poor academic performance	-Lack of proper guidance -Risks involved in educating girls
No. of districts	7	4	4
Issue thus rated	N.A	N.A	-Teenage pregnancy
Local educational leaders (N=268)	-Irregular school attendance and -Poor academic performance	-Parental/ Community poverty and child labor	-Irregular school attendance and poor academic performance
No. of districts	4	4	5
Issue thus rated	-Teenage pregnancy and early marriages	-Teenage pregnancy and early marriages	N.A
No. of districts	4	3	-

Thus in only three districts did teachers perceive harsh and insecure environment and lack of adequate and proper guidance particularly for girls, respectively, as the second most important causes of dropout from school. Similarly, local educational administrators in four districts mentioned parental/community poverty, often leading to child labor, as the second most important cause of dropout from school. Local educational administrators in three districts identified the second most salient cause of dropout from school to be teenage pregnancy and early marriage among girls.

In only four districts, head teachers identified irregular school attendance resulting in poor academic performance as the second most important cause of quitting schooling.   Among local educational administrators, two factors tied for second place, namely parental/community poverty and teenage pregnancy resulting in early marriage. The first factor was identified to be important in four districts while the second received mention in three districts (see Table 5.10).

As is apparent in Table 5.10 there were more consensuses within each category/educational personnel regarding the third most important cause of dropping out from school. Among teachers in five districts and head teachers in four districts, it was lack of adequate and proper guidance especially resulting in disadvantages for girls.   Lastly, among local educational administrators in five districts, the third most important cause of dropout from school among pupils was given as irregular attendance of school resulting in poor academic performance among pupils.   There should be no denying that irregular school attendance and poor academic performance especially among girls may in fact be related to lack of adequate and appropriate guidance. In this sense the two factors identified by educational personnel, cited in this study, as third most important in causing dropout from school by pupils may be regarded as merely two faces of the same coin.

Overall, the educational personnel in Kenya, according to the survey of 1994, appeared singularly consistent in their perceptions of the three leading candidates among causes of dropout from primary school. In terms of the districts in which the issues were mentioned, the salient factors in school dropout rated overall as shown in Table 5.11.

Table 5.11 Overall Rating of Salient Causes of School Dropout

Causes	Number of District in which salient
- Parental/community poverty	18
- Irregular attendance of school/poor performance	13
- Lack of adequate/proper guidance	12
- Teenage pregnancy/early marriage	10

In essence, therefore, these are the four factors that any measures to improve retention of pupils in Kenyan primary schools must take into account. The next chapter examines the measures which educational personnel proposed as means for ameliorating non-enrolment, class repetition and dropout from school. The proposed solutions are presented sequentially for each dimension of educational wastage.

6 Identified Solutions for Each Component of Wastage

In the preceding chapter, attention was focused on the major causes of non-enrolment, class repetition and dropout from primary school education. A major cause was recognized as that cause which was identified by at least 10 per cent of those to whom the question regarding causes of each educational wastage component was posed. Through a sieving process, only three of the most important causes of each educational wastage component were highlighted and earmarked for possible remedial action.

In this chapter, solutions proposed to handle the identified causes of wastage in education are presented, first in broad outline and, second, in terms of the three most important remedies. Solutions, which meet the last criterion are those mentioned by at least 10 per cent of the respondents and rated from first to third in importance. Sequentially, therefore, we examine those remedies that were identified in respect to the causes of non-enrolment, class repetition and school dropout.

Perceived Solutions for Non-Enrolment

Information solicited from the three cadres of educational personnel who were interviewed revealed a wide range of views regarding possible remedies for non-enrolment in primary school education. The more widely mentioned remedies are shown in Table 6.1.

The proposed solutions reflect programs, which are community specific and those that are school-linked. The measures that touch directly on community initiative were based on a number of preconditions. These include the need to mobilize and sensitize some parents and communities generally on the importance of schooling for their children; the need for the government policy makers to legislate for and implement free and compulsory primary schooling or to reduce school levies; the need to give parents and community members income generating capabilities (economic empowerment); and the

93

need to supply basic services to schools and neighboring communities. Measures that are school specific embrace the provision of primary boarding schools especially in favor of girls; the provision of more learning facilities and resources for pupils; and the need to organize school feeding (lunch) programs for pupils.

Table 6.1   Proposed Solutions for Non-Enrolment

1: Mobilize and sensitize parents and community on importance of schooling.
2: Provide additional primary boarding schools especially for girls.
3: Provide bursaries or scholarships for needy children.
4: Legislate for free and compulsory education or reduce school-related levies.
5: Provide more learning facilities and resources.
6: Economically empower parents and communities.
7: Provide basic services such as health, water and food for schools and surrounding communities.
8: Organise school feeding programs for pupils.

Ranking of the proposed solutions for non-enrolment on the basis of frequency of mentions, which is a measure of the salience of the particular issues among the groups that were surveyed yielded the results shown in Table 6.2.

The table shows ranking in terms of the three most important possible remedies to non-enrolment proposed by each of the three categories of educational staff that were covered in the study on wastage in primary school education. The results show a remarkable consensus between teachers and local educational administrators on the point that mobilizing and sensitizing parents and other members of the community about the importance of schooling is by far the most important strategy in efforts to reduce non-enrolment (increase enrolment). Interestingly, head teachers do not perceive this strategy to reduce non-enrolment as important. Thus, nowhere did ten per cent or more of the head teachers mention this remedy at all.

Table 6.2   **Frequencies of Mentions of Ordered Proposed Remedies for Non-Enrolment by the Three Categories of Ministry of Education Staff**

	Ranking of Proposed Remedies		
Category of Staff	Most important	Second most important	Third most important
Teachers (N=1495)	Mobilise and sensitize community/ parents	Provide free and compulsory education	Provide free and compulsory education
No. of districts	9	6	3
Head teachers (N=172)	Provide boarding schools mainly for girls	Provide boarding schools mainly for girls	Provide bursaries and scholarships for Needy Children
No. of districts	5	3	4
Local educational leaders (N=268)	Mobilise and sensitize Community/ Parents	Mobilize and sensitise community/ parents	Economically empower parents/communities.
No. of districts	6	2	4
Issue mentioned	Provide more learning resources and facilities	N.A	N.A
No. of districts	2	-	-

Instead, head teachers who were interviewed rated the need to provide boarding schools especially for girls as the most important corrective measure to non-enrolment in school. Table 6.2 shows that this measure received priority rating among head teachers in five out of the ten districts that were studied.

It is also noted that in two districts, local educational administrators rated the provision of more learning facilities and resources as the leading means to increase enrolment in school. None of the other educational personnel shown in Table 6.2 mentioned this remedy at all among the three most important possibilities. It appears that local educational administrators were of the view that other stakeholders in education besides the Government needed to play their role in expanding educational opportunities for children. In the context of the policy of cost-sharing that one witnesses in Kenya, local educational leaders, as representatives of the Kenyan Government at grassroots level, were proposing a number of measures: first that communities and other stakeholders should put up additional classrooms; second, that they should provide to pupils school textbooks and other learning resources; and third, that communities and other stake holders should provide school feeding programs for children. These measures would hopefully make education accessible and attractive to as many children as possible.

In the view of teachers who were surveyed, the second most important strategy to increase enrolment in primary schools was through the provision of free and compulsory education. The teachers also rate this measure as the third most important strategy to compensate for the inability by many children to enroll in school. The responses of both head teachers and local educational administrators as shown in Table 6.2 reveal differences with teachers regarding measures that were rated as second most important in handling non-enrolment in school. For head teachers this was given as the provision of boarding schools targeting mainly girls. Among local educational leaders the comparative remedy was mobilisation and sensitisation of parents and other community members on the benefits of education for their children. The three categories of educational personnel therefore gave distinctly different measures as being the second most important in ameliorating non-enrolment.

On the face of it, the third most important strategy identified by each group of educational personnel to address the problem of non-enrolment in school appears different. A careful examination, however, shows that all three measures address parental or guardian ability to meet the financial and related costs of education for their children. Teachers are of the view that more children will be attracted to join schooling when legislation for free and compulsory primary school education permits their parents or guardians to take them to school. This situation would allow children free access to schooling on the one hand and make it obligatory for parents or guardians to enroll their children in school on the other hand. For head teachers, a very similar outcome would be achieved through the provision of scholarships and bursaries to economically disadvantaged children. The proposal of local educational leaders appears more long-term as it calls for initiating and supporting income-generating projects for needy parents and members of different communities. Once these parents and other individuals in the community are economically able they will have the capability to pay various school charges. Implementing measures suggested by this strategy is a long-term process in the sense that sponsors must be identified, finances mobilized and recipients of funds trained in business and financial management and then encouraged to implement their business projects.

Since our premise was that all issues rated between 1 and 3 were salient and therefore constitute the focus of policy decisions, a summary of all mentions received by each proposed measure gives an indication of its ultimate importance. From the data in Table 6.2, the various corrective measures for non-enrolment in school are ranked, in terms of number of mentions in the ten districts, as shown in Table 6.3.

Table 6.3   Summary Ranking of Measures to Correct Non-Enrolment

Measures	Number of Districts Issue Salient
Mobilize and sensitize parents	17
Free and compulsory education	9
Provision of Bursaries and scholarships	4
Economically empower communities/parents	4
Provide more learning facilities and resources	2
Provide boarding schools, particularly for girls	8

The summary results in the box reaffirm the leading importance of the strategy of mobilizing and sensitizing parents and the various community members about the importance or benefits of schooling for their children. Four strategies collectively share an underlying concern with relieving parents, especially poor ones, from the financial burden of educating their children. This concern, whether it takes the form of free and compulsory education, access to bursaries or scholarships or economic improvement for parents and members of communities, requires the attention of policy makers who are interested in increasing enrolment in primary school by children. The other, and final salient measure in improving enrolment in primary school education is the provision of public boarding schools particularly for girls. Parents and educational personnel interviewed felt that the current policy where Government supports only primary schools that are day schools should be re-examined. This situation seems to prevent many children, especially girls, from enrolling in primary school education.

Having thus examined the measures that were proposed to tackle non-enrolment in primary schooling, we turn in the next section to measures, which informants in our study on educational wastage offered as strategies for overcoming class or grades repetition.

Solutions Proposed for Class Repetition

Table 6.4 presents the kinds of remedies that were proposed by the surveyed teachers, head teachers and local educational administrators to reduce class repetition. It is perhaps not surprising that four out of the eight suggested remedies for class repetition touch upon activities in which the education system and personnel are likely to be the major actors. The four proposed remedies referred to here include the provision of more learning resources and facilities; encouraging pupils to attend school regularly; encouraging greater support for pupils by both teachers and parents; and the need to improve teacher quality through in-service training. The first three of these activities would require the involvement of other stakeholders outside the school such as parents, the government, religious agencies as well as Non-Governmental Organizations. Nonetheless, the major impetus for action on these measures would have to come from school authorities including parents-teachers associations and school committees.

The fourth remedy, improvement of teacher quality and teaching through in-service training and related programs, is largely a matter for school authorities themselves. In the Kenyan context, the key actors would have to include the offices of the Provincial Directors of Education and the District Education Offices (DEOs), the Kenya Education Staff Institute (KESI), personnel of Teachers Advisory Centres (TACs), local educational inspectors and individual head teachers. Certainly, improved pedagogy has the potential to sustain the interest and enthusiasm of pupils in learning and thus their retention in school.

Table 6.4 Perceived Solutions for Class Repetition

1: Mobilize and sensitize parents and community on importance of schooling.

2: Review the primary school curriculum.

3: Provide more learning resources and facilities.

4: Encourage pupils to attend school regularly.

5: Economically empower parents and communities.

6: Provide boarding schools particularly for girls.

7: Encourage greater support for pupils by both teachers and parents.

8: Improve teacher quality and teaching through in-service training/courses.

The remaining four among the eight proposed remedies that require action mainly from non-school authorities are mobilization and sensitization of parents and communities on the importance of schooling; review of the primary school curriculum; provision of more boarding schools particularly for girls; and enhancing the economic capability of parents and other community members. Since in Kenya, as in most other African countries, school curricula are determined and formulated by the state, reviewing the primary school curriculum would have to involve political leaders and key senior government administrators. Included among such actors would be senior officers in the Ministry of Education, but only as part of a much larger and perhaps more influential team.

Similarly, mobilization and sensitization of communities on the benefits of schooling, and channeling economic projects to individuals and communities, are largely political acts. That is, they require the active involvement of political functionaries such as local politicians and administrators and often national political personalities as well. Even where internal agencies and some Non-Governmental Organizations are involved as facilitators, they are bound to work within the framework set by national leaders and key administrators.

Lastly, the proposal regarding the establishment of public boarding primary schools in some areas and targeting girls in particular, may be initiated by educational leaders but must be sold to both local and national political elites if such activities are to obtain the necessary legitimacy.

Separating young children, and especially girls, from their parents is a sensitive issue that is bound to involve considerable tactical persuasion. The program is at the same time costly financially and the state treasury officials need to be convinced that the benefits of primary boarding schools would more than offset the costs.

While outlining the remedial measures proposed for class repetition is useful, what is more important is to decipher which of the eight proposed remedies received significant rating. This brings us again to the criterion regarding decisions about the three most important rankings among the measures that were identified. The results on the basis of the established criterion are summarized in Table 6.5 for each category of educational staff surveyed.

A few key observations can be made in reference to the results in the table. First, that for both teachers and head teachers the most important way of reducing class repetition is through getting parents and communities to have a positive and deep interest in the education of their children. In this way parents and other community members can be expected to provide the necessary inputs required for the education of the children. It is in this respect relevant that the most important measure proposed by local educational administrators to handle the issue of class repetition, namely encouraging regular attendance of school by pupils, is an integral part of community mobilization and sensitization. Getting children to regularly attend school requires parental and community concern and willingness to ensure attendance; it, of course, also involves teachers insisting on and monitoring school attendance by pupils. But the real push for regular attendance of school by pupils must first come from households in which the children live.

Table 6.5 **Frequencies of Mentions of Ordered Proposed Remedies for Repetition by the Three Categories of Ministry of Education Staff**

	Ranking of Proposed Remedies		
Category of staff	Most important	Second most important	Third most important
Teachers (N=1495)	Mobilize and sensitize community/ parents	Review of current Kenyan curriculum	Ensuring pupil's attendance regularly
Head teachers (N=172)	Mobilize and sensitive community/ parents	Improve the quality of learning facilities and resources	Support pupils through supervision by both teachers and parents. Boarding school for girls
Local education al leaders (N=268)	Ensuring pupils attendance regularly	Review of current Kenyan school curriculum	Improving quality of learning facilities. improving economic status of parents.

On the second most important remedy for class repetition, teachers and local educational administrators concur that this should take the form of review of the current Kenyan primary school curriculum. The current primary school curriculum is known as the 8-4-4 curriculum that stands for 8 years of primary school education, 4 years of secondary school education and a minimum of 4 years of University education. It was launched in 1985 and replaced the 7-4-2-3 system that had represented 7 years of primary school education, 4 years of secondary education, 2 years of senior secondary school ('A' level) and 3 years of minimum university education.

The 8-4-4 system of education has regularly been criticized by educationists, politicians and the general public for a number of reasons. The major ones include the hurried way in which it was launched, the many new subjects it introduced at every level of education, and nostalgia for the allegedly superior system education it replaced. There is a large number of individuals and groups who believe that a review of the 8-4-4 curriculum, particularly reduction of the number of subjects offered, would increase enthusiasm for schooling, improve academic performance and thus reduce class repetition.

For head teachers, the second most important strategy to reduce class or grade repetition was perceived to be increasing the amount and improving the quality of learning facilities and resources. Consensus among head teachers on this proposal was witnessed in three of the ten districts surveyed. Although this represents a low level of salience, the point remains important that the acquisition of quality learning resources provides a good basis for improving learning achievement and therefore reducing class repetition due to poor academic performance. In a fundamental sense, therefore, head teachers appear to be supporting the proposal of both teachers and local educational administrators that measures which improve the quality of learning, are important in reducing repetition.

There were fewer consensuses among the three categories of educational staff regarding the third most important measure to reduce class repetition. Teachers in five out of the ten districts studied expressed the view that grade repetition can better be curtailed by ensuring that pupils attend school regularly in order to adequately follow lessons. It will be recalled that local educational leaders proposed this as the leading measure in possible strategies to reduce class repetition by pupils.

For head teachers, two measures were identified in two different districts as being the third most important in reducing class repetition. These were supporting the academic work of pupils through supervision by both teachers and parents; and providing more boarding schools especially to cater for girls. These are two separate and distinct strategies for ameliorating class repetition.

Local educational leaders proposed two additional remedial measures for grade repetition. These two were the provision of more learning resources and facilities in schools; and improving the economic status of parents and other relevant members of the community to enable them to afford the costs associated with educating the children. It can be admitted that where parents and other members of a community are economically well off, they are likely to provide more and better learning facilities and resources. The two proposals made by local educational leaders here are therefore linked, especially since this group of educational staff usually promote the

Government policy of cost-sharing. An important component of this policy is that parents and communities shoulder responsibility for the provision of physical facilities and basic learning resources in schools while the Government pays teachers' salaries and allowances.

In sum, while a variety of measures were proposed to deal with class repetition, we can cumulatively arrive at the most salient three on the basis of the number of times they were mentioned by sampled informants. Since all issues mentioned were already among the most important, a pooled score indicates the more salient of the issues. Table 6.6 gives the cumulative ranking of the various proposals.

The evidence in the box reveals that the three most salient measures which should be considered in combating class or grade repetition. These include the mobilization and sensitization of parents and other members of the community about the importance of schooling for children; encouraging pupils to attend school regularly; and periodic review of the primary school curriculum. While the need to provide more learning resources and facilities is important in improving student learning and therefore reducing repetition due to poor performance in examinations, the measure ranks a distant fourth. Nonetheless it may be easier and more effective to attend to this measure than to review the primary school curriculum. Reviewing an education system's curriculum is a very sensitive political activity and also economically very expensive. This is not to say that curriculum review should not be done, only that it should be undertaken on careful reflection regarding the costs and benefits.

In the section that follows, attention shifts to a discussion of solutions which were proposed to ameliorate dropout from primary school education. In making the presentation, it be will helpful to pay particular attention to which of the solutions lie within the control of the school system, which ones fall outside the school system and which ones require action of both educational and community leaders.

Table 6.6   Cumulative Rating of Measures to Reduce Repetition

Cause	Number of Districts in which Salient
1: Mobilize and sensitize parents and communities.	18
2: Encourage regular attendance.	8
3: Review curriculum.	9
4: Provide more resources.	5
5: Provide boarding facilities.	2
6: Parental and school support for pupils.	2
7: Economically empower parents and communities.	2

Measures Proposed to Reduce Dropout

The measures proposed by the three categories of educational personnel namely teachers, head teachers and local educational administrators, to reduce dropout from school, were more than those proposed for non-enrolment and class repetition. In all, ten remedies were proposed and these are shown in Table 6.7. As was the case regarding the causes of this aspect of educational wastage, most of the proposed remedies as shown in Table 6.7 span the within school and out of school interactive matrix. Six of the ten remedies qualify in this respect. They are the provision of more learning facilities and resources; encouragement of closer cooperation between the school and the surrounding community in which the school is located; the provision of bursaries and scholarships for needy children; encouraging pupils to attend school regularly; and making available more boarding schools for some pupils especially girls. And finally, the reduction of charges levied by schools.

All the mentioned six measures require action involving school personnel and other educational operatives as well as the members of the wider communities. Irrespective of which party initiates the activity, both educationalists and community leaders and members have to be part of the reform action.

Three of the proposed remedies shown in Table 6.7 fall more decidedly within the sphere of influence of the community. Included within this category are mobilization and sensitization of parents and other individuals in the communities on the importance of schooling for children; reduction of workload (household chores) for girls at home; and improving the economic welfare (empowerment) of parents and other members of various communities. On all three instances, initiative for action rests more with communities and especially community leaders. This is not to say that some of the educational personnel may not be involved in implementing these proposed remedies. They may be actively involved, but only as actors co-opted by the leaders and members of the communities outside the schools.

Only one remedy proposed by the educational personnel, improving teaching and providing remedial teaching to learners was specific to the school system itself. In other words, school personnel within the school system can implement the proposed measure without support from elsewhere save from educational administrators. The Ministry of Education in Kenya, as elsewhere, may have to establish policy guidelines, but once this framework is available, actual implementation of remedial teaching for academically weak pupils will be the direct responsibility of the individual schools.

Table 6.7   Proposed Solutions for Dropout

1. Provision of more learning facilities and resources.
2. Closer cooperation between school and surrounding community.
3. Provision of bursaries and scholarships for needy children.
4. Encouraging peoples to attend school regularly.
5. Building more boarding schools especially for girls.
6. Reduction of charges levied by the school.
7. Mobilization and sensitization of parents to the importance of schooling.
8. Reduction of work-load for girls at home.
9. Improving the living standards of parents.
10. Improving teaching and providing remedial teaching to peoples.

Rating of the ten proposed remedies in terms of the three most important ones is shown in Table 6.8. It is clear that for both teachers and local educational administrators, the leading solution to dropout from school was identified as community mobilization and sensitization on the need to retain children in school until they complete the specific educational cycle. For head teachers, the leading solution was identified as the provision of more learning facilities and resources. These two proposals while different should be regarded as complementary. Certainly, one useful strategy of retaining pupils in school is to ensure that they have adequate learning facilities and resources that make meaningful learning possible and enjoyable.

The results presented in the table also suggest great heterogeneity among teachers regarding the second most important remedy for dropout from school. This is confirmed by mention among this cadre of educational personnel of four measures, in two districts each, as the second most important corrective to dropout. Two of the suggested remedies namely the provision of more learning facilities and resources and improvement in teaching especially in the form of remedial teaching for slow learners, are complementary. Improved teaching of which remedial teaching is a component makes better sense in the context of adequate availability of quality learning facilities and resources.

The other measure in the form of greater cooperation between the school and the community is similar to what teachers rated as the most important remedy for dropout from school, the mobilization and sensitization of parents and communities on the importance of schooling. Closer cooperation between the school and the community may in fact bring about a greater awareness of what goes on in schools on the part of the community; and the school authorities and pupils also stand a better chance of appreciating communities, expectations of beneficial schooling outcomes.

While the provision of bursaries or scholarships to needy pupils may in fact be facilitated by greater school-community approachment, the initiative for such a scheme belongs properly to the Government through the Ministry of Education. The only exception is where influential local (or community) elites come together to sponsor such scholarships and bursaries.

Head teachers and local educational administrators showed more consensuses in respect of the second most important remedy for dropout from school. In three districts a significant proportion of head teachers (greater than 10%) identified the second most important solution to dropping out of school to be mobilization and sensitization of parents and other community members. In the case of local educational administrators, the second most important solution to school dropout was identified in four districts as improvement in the economic conditions of parents and other community members. This last remedy does underscore awareness of local educational administrators that parental and communal poverty is a great impediment to retention of children in Kenyan schools where education is neither compulsory nor free.

Table 6.8 **Frequencies of Mentions of Ordered Proposed Solutions to Dropout by the Three Categories of Ministry of Education Staff**

	Ranking of Proposed remedies		
Category of staff	Most important	Second most important	Third most important
Teachers (N=1495)	Mobilize and sensitize parents and community (8 districts)	More learning resources and facilities (2 districts)	Provide bursaries and scholarships for needy children (2 districts)
	N.A	Greater School community cooperation (2 districts)	N.A
	N.A	Provide Bursaries and scholarships for needy children (2 districts)	N.A
	N.A	Improve teaching, Provide remedial Teaching(2 districts)	N.A
Head teachers (N=268)	Provide more learning resources and facilities (5 districts)	Mobilize and sensitize parents and community (3 districts)	Reduce work load for girls at household level (4 districts)
Local educational leaders (N=268)	Mobilize and sensitize parents and community (8 districts)	Economically empower parents and communities (4 districts)	Encourage regular attendance of school by pupils (3 districts)

Perhaps teachers also underscored the need to address the issue of poverty among parents and communities from which pupils come, in proposing that the third most important palliative to school dropout was the provision of bursaries and/or scholarships to needy children. This was the perception of teachers in two of the districts covered in the survey.

The third most important remedy to dropping out of school among head teachers was the need to give girls light household chores so that they would be in a position to attend better to school learning tasks. In a fundamental sense, this proposal tallies very well with teachers' earlier suggestion that there should be greater cooperation between the school and the community. It is largely in the context this cooperation that one sees good prospects of persuading parents to alleviate household workload for their daughters who are enrolled in school.

In the case of local educational leaders, the third most important remedy for dropout from school was perceived as regular attendance of school by pupils. This remedy was viewed as important in three districts. It can be appreciated that irregular attendance of school by pupils may arise from little valuation for schooling by parents and, by extension, the pupils themselves; this condition may also result from poverty which forces pupils to stay away because they are unable to pay full amounts demanded by school authorities or they have to work to supplement family incomes, an activity which eats into their time for attending school.

In a real sense, all the remedies outlined thus far were important on the basis of our criteria that they were identified by more than ten (10) per cent of each category of respondents within a district. Nonetheless, the results in Table 6.9 allow for a polled evaluation of these important proposed remedies. This is done by summing up the number of districts in which particular remedial measures are mentioned by all three categories of educational staff.

We present in Table 6.9 the results of such a cumulative rating.

Table 6.9   Overall Rating of the Proposed Remedies to School Dropout

Solution	Number of Districts in which salient
1: Mobilize and sensitize parents on benefits of education for children.	19
2: Provide more and quality learning facilities and resources.	9
3: Provide bursaries and scholarships.	4
4: Reduce domestic workload for girls.	4
5: Improve economic conditions of parents and other community members.	4

The results confirm the outstanding importance of the strategy, which calls for parental, and community mobilization and sensitization on the importance of education for their children. This finding illustrates rather forcefully that educational leaders who were surveyed shift responsibility for dropout from school by pupils to members of the communities from which such children come.

The second, but distant, proposal is the provision of more learning facilities and resources. The conventional thinking at the time of the survey was that parents and communities are the ones expected to provide the bulk of the 'new' facilities and resources. The Government's role is only to supplement community efforts where justified. In this respect as well, solutions to dropout from school were placed largely at the doorsteps of the communities and not of educational leaders.

When it came to proposal that may require greater Government inputs, the educational personnel were clearly less forthcoming. This is attested to by the relatively few districts in which mention was made of the need for the Government to provide scholarships or bursaries for needy children, and to institute measures that would lead to economic improvement for parents and other community members. These two remedies, and the need to reduce workload for girls enrolled in school, were cumulatively salient in only four (4) districts. This pattern of findings is also further evidence of the heterogeneity that characterized the perceptions of the three cadres of educational staff on the possible remedies of school dropout. In fact, the third most important measure to deal with school dropout was indeterminate among the three cadres of educational staff.

7 Profiles of Selected Initiatives to Reduce Wastage

This chapter presents the results of the evaluation studies of projects in terms of: (a) background information including the rationale for their establishment, the intended beneficiaries and the sponsors; (b) the specific objectives of the projects and their organizational structures; and (c) project activities or services and the costs of operating the projects where this kind of information is available. The format presented here is applied to projects within the framework of the five broad types of initiatives that were identified for the evaluation study.

Health and Nutrition Initiatives

Background and Rationale

Three Health and Nutrition initiatives are examined here. These are the Bamko Initiative Centers (BICs) in Baringo districts, the National School Feeding Council of Kenya program in Kiambu and Nyeri Districts.

The Bamko initiative is a UNICEF strategy for expanded implementation of primary health care conceived by the African Health Ministers, WHO Regional Committee and UNICEF in Bamako, Mali, in 1987. The initiative was an offshoot of WHO's declaration on health for all by the year 2000.

In principle, Bamako initiatives are usually located in areas with limited access to health facilities and with attendant high prevalence of such preventable diseases as malaria, yellow fever, eye infection, worm infection, and diarrhoeal diseases. Kisumu and Baringo are characterized by these problems.

In Kisumu district, morbidity rates around 50 percent and child mortality rate of 199 per 1000 live births have been reported. Water-borne diseases and malaria infections account for the bulk of child-deaths in this district. For Baringo district, major contributors to poor health include a hostile topography which has hampered the development of a good transportation network, the standing waters of lake Baringo and Bogoria, and large areas without access to both adequate and quality water resources. In consequence, few of the inhabitants of this district have access to the health facilities located mainly along the few roads with good transportation. Like in Kisumu, malaria and water-borne diseases are common epidemics in Baringo district.

UNICEF has usually had a visible presence in Kenyan districts with high infant mortality and high rates of child morbidity. Kisumu and Baringo were two of the country's seven or so districts that received preferential health Programs from UNICEF Kenya in the 1980s and 1990s. The Kisumu BIC's were started as a pilot project in 1988. The initiative was extended to Baringo district four years later 1992. In both situations, the initiatives were started as a response to widespread inaccessibility to medical facilities and services, and high incidence of child morbidity and mortality. The broad goal of the Barmoko initiative was to strengthen community based activities directed mainly to improving the quality of life and survival of women and children.

The major sponsors of the BICs in Kenya have been UNICEF and Canadian International Development Agency (CIDA). There have also been supplementary donors, which include the African Medical Research Foundation (AMRF), Aga Khan Foundation and Care-Kenya. The Ministry of Health lays a tutelage role in the form of supervision and monitoring of BICs activities.

The national School feeding Program evaluated in Kiambu and Nyeri districts, covers schools in twelve other districts. These other districts are Kirimgaga and Muranga in central province, Embu, Meru, Machasws and Kitui in eastern province, Nandi and Kisuku in Rift valley and Nyanza Provinces, respectively; a few schools are also catered for in the Nairobi province. The total number of schools served in 1995 was 355. The program was initiated in 1967 under the auspices of the National School Feeding Council of Kenya, to supplement pupil's diet in schools in a few selected districts. The central goal of the School Feeding Council is the improvement of the nutritional status of preschool and primary school children through the provision, at minimal cost, of a morning drink and a mid-day supplementary meal during school hours.

The school feeding program grew out of a survey by the Ministry of Education and WHO in 1963/64, which revealed poor nutritional status among children attending primary school in Kenya. This finding contradicted the Universal Declaration of Human Rights of 1948, which stipulated that freedom from hunger and malnutrition was a basic human right. The Ministry of Education and WHO accordingly deliberated on possible solutions to the problem revealed by the survey and proposed a school based program that would pilot a morning drink and school lunches to supplement the Vitamin and Protein intake of young school children.

OXFAM, a British Non-Governmental Organization (NGO), was approached to fund and supervise a two-year pilot program in six districts of Embu, Kiambu, Kilifi, Kwale, Taita-Taveta and Tharaka. The program was found viable and was therefore poised to gain national coverage. But the program never gained national status. Today the School Feeding Program is run by National School Feeding Council of Kenya. It does so on account of strong backing in the provision of food items by parents and management by joint committees of parents and teachers.

Objectives and Organizational Structure

The Bamako initiatives have very specific objectives in their areas of operation. From official sources, the objectives of this kind of initiative were given as: a) To sensitize the community about health issues; b) To provide the community with some basic facilities and services such as pharmacy, drugs and mosquito nets; c) To assist communities in improving sanitation and water services; d) To enhance child survival and development; e) To raise the living standard for the community through proper health care; f) To provide additional health services in the district.

The outlined objectives were intended primarily to meet the needs of women and children, who have traditionally been at the center of UNICEF's activities. BICs also extended a few services such as the provision of drugs and mosquito nets to other members of the communities in which they are located. The contribution of BICs to the welfare of school children is through the improvement of their health, which is expected to produce pay offs in the form of better school attendance and learning gains.

In terms of organizational structure, the Bamako Initiatives at Kisumu and Baringo are strikingly similar. The heads of the program are in Kisumu town, which is the provincial headquarters. The head of the Bamako program in Baringo is the UNICEF District Officer based in Kabarnet town, the district headquarters. Both consult with the Ministry of Health Senior Officers in their areas of operation and the UNICEF Kenya country office in Nairobi; and they are directly accountable to the latter organization.

While the activities of the Bamako Initiative Centers (BICs) are coordinated from the Kisumu and Baringo UNICEF Regional Offices, respectively, the management of day-to- day activities of these centers is very decentralized. Apart from overall coordination the regional office in either district assists the communities in carrying out needs assessment surveys and in formulating plans of action and training various cadre of community health workers.

Each BIC is principally managed by the respective communities through various village committees. The most central of these is the village health committee whose membership includes a chairman and vice-chairman, secretary and vice-secretary, a treasurer and a number of committee members. Committee members are in fact selected from persons who work in health related activities. To this end, committee membership incorporated village health workers, trainees of trainers, traditional birth attendants and pharmacy attendants.

In serving school children, the National School Feeding Program has a complimentary role to health efforts made by programs like BICs. The broad aim of the Feeding Program is the improvement of the nutritional status and consequently the health status of pre-school and primary children. In focusing on school children, the National School Feeding Program seeks to promote a number of objectives, the major ones which include: a) Supplementing the diets of children who usually have little food in their homes; b) Easing the burden of children whose homes are far from school and would therefore waste too much time traveling between school and home for lunch; c) Saving some time during lunch break to enable pupils and teachers to cover an already overloaded primary syllabus; d) Freeing parents, who are often too busy, from an extra responsibility of preparing lunch for their school going children; e) Alleviation of the problem of hunger and malnutrition among primary school children; f) Increasing enrolment in schools especially of children from poor communities in both urban and rural areas; g) Maintenance of regular attendance of school by pupils; h) Improvement in the quality of learning by ensuring good concentration during afternoon classes by pupils who are not hungry; i) Improvement in academic performance by pupils.

As can be gauged from most of the objectives listed, the orientation of the National School Feeding Program is strongly educational. The central purpose of making lunch available is to enhance the participation of children in education with the end aim of improving academic performance by the pupils. The school children the program targets are those from low-income households in middle and high economic potential districts in the country. Children in the low potential districts, mainly to be found in arid and semi arid lands, were already being catered for by the World Food Program (WFP).

The National School Feeding Council of Kenya had initiated to provide at least 30% of school children at risk from malnutrition in the middle and high school potential districts, with food. High on the agenda were orphans and children of single parents most of the latter being single mothers. A fundamental point is that once a program such the National School Feeding, involves cost-sharing with parents, mainly the more economically able ones will tend to be involved in its activities. Our survey of the feeding program in Kiamba and Nyeri reveals a defacto distortion in the original objective of having it cater solely for children from economically depressed households. Increasingly, the program caters for children whose parents or guardians are able to afford the costs associated with supporting feeding for school children. Those whose parents are unable to meet such costs are, ipso facto, excluded from the feeding program. Many of these excluded children are from poor households.

The organizational structure of the studied National School Feeding Program is simple. At the top of the administrative arrangement is the National School Feeding Council Executive Committee whose membership includes at least one representative of the original founder organizations namely, The National Council of Churches of Kenya, The Catholic Secretariat, Kenya National Council of Social Services, National Council of Women of Kenya, Kenya National Union of Teachers, African Medical Research Foundation, Catholic Relief Services, Save the Children Fund, Kenya Red Cross, Christian Churches Education Association, Child Welfare Society of Kenya, and Kenya Freedom From Hunger Council.

A District School Feeding Program Council of Kenya field officer represents the national organization at the district level. This officer works with a District Committee consisting of parents- Teachers Association, the development Officer, the District Health Officer and a few co-opted leading personalities in the District. This district level committee is responsible for the arrangement and monitoring of the program and for popularizing it among parents. The District Committee works with a number of school based lunch committees which consist of representatives of teachers and parents. In fact it is these school lunch committees, working in collaboration with school administration, that run the school feeding program on a day to day basis within each participating school. Each school lunch committee consults with the National School Feeding Council District field officer on transactions such as the purchase and supply of food intended for the target school children.

Program Activities and Services

Activities associated with Health and Nutrition Initiative are expected to have an impact on problems of educational wastage. That is, what is it that programs which fall under Health and Nutrition Initiative provide to children that lead many of them to join school, to matriculate between grades or standards without repeating one or more of the grades and to complete the full cycle of the educational tier in which they have enrolled?

To start with, the two Bamako Initiatives that were investigated, focused mainly on the health and health related activities. Specifically, there were four components to these programs which included: a) health care; b) water and sanitation; c) Social Services; and d) education.

The health activities clustered around the BICs pharmacy. The pharmacy sells drugs to members of the community at subsidized prices. Also sold cheaply to the community are mosquito nets to reduce incidents of mosquito bites and therefore the risk of malaria infection. At the pharmacy, immunization, growth monitoring de-worming and eye-check-ups for children have also been conducted. The staff of the BICs, through public meetings (called barazas in Kiswahili,) have sensitized members of the community on a variety of health issues including control and treatment of diseases. UNICEF has been the main supplier of funds and other resources for these activities. Money accruing from sale of some of the products is put in a revolving fund to sustain the services.

CIDA, a co-sponsor of the Bamako Initiatives in Kenya, has strongly supported the second component of activities, the provision of water and sanitation. CIDA has ensured a steady supply of such materials as iron-sheets, cement, water pipes and water tanks. The community has utilized these resources in the construction of water wells and water pipes, harvesting of rain water and building of toilets.

The third constellation of activities have focused on the provision of such social services as gender sensitization seminars and workshops, and encouragement of adult members of the community to facilitate the registration of births and deaths. Gender sensitization seminars have included, as one of the main messages, equitable treatment of girls by reducing their involvement in household chores, and thus freeing time for them to study.

In the area of education services, the Bamako Initiative has relied on sensitization meetings (barazas) to get parents to enroll children in pre-schools and primary schools. A few of the BICs have put up nursery schools as demonstration projects which other communities can replicate in or near their areas of residence.

The financial costs of providing the various Bamako Initiative Services were, like those of many activities associated with the other four types of initiative, difficult to obtain either directly from key project informants, or project records. Project personnel were generally reluctant to disclose information on costs of their activities and services. Nonetheless, some figures on costs provided for the Bamako Initiative in Kisumu gives a rough indication of the level of funds required to run this kind of program. Table 7.1 carries relevant data.

Table 7.1   Costs of Operating Activities of Kisumu Bamako Initiative (1995)

Activity line	Cost in Millions (Kenya Shillings)
Health Care	8.0
Immunization	8.0
Water/Sanitation materials	14.0
Social Services	6.0
Education Services	3.0
NGO activities	10.0
Fuel/petrol	4.0
Total	53.0

The costs of running the Bamako Initiative's activities are quite high. Of the total cost, members of the community shoulder about 30 per cent which in this case amounts to about Kenya shillings 15.9 million annually. Much of this payment is in-kind consisting of contribution of land for the construction of water wells and pharmacies, contribution of labor, food and other pooled resources. Whatever form the contributions take, what is clear is that there is a heavy financial out-lay required for various program activities.

The next point to discuss are the activities and services undertaken by the National School Feeding Program in Kiambu and Nyeri Disrticts. In many respects, the functions of this initiative are more focused than the Bamako one. Essentially, this nutrition initiative provides feeding for school children, supplies the kitchen equipment and energy resources required in the preparation of food, and promotes some nutrition and health education among parents of school children. Each school lunch committee within the program purchases and prepares food for participating children.

The cost of running the National School Feeding Programs in Kiambu and Nyeri were not easy to determine. This was partly the case because some activities such as the purchase distribution and preparation of food are subsidized by Kenya Government Grants while administrative costs of paying staff and purchase and maintenance of kitchen equipment are usually subsidized by one or two major donors. Also the Head Office in Nairobi handled every aspect of the budget. Faced with this kind of situation, information obtained on costs of running the school nutrition program was sketchy and rudimentary.

For instance, the most that was revealed by fieldwork was that in 1995 it cost a family an average of Kenya Shillings 300 a month (about US$5) to support a child in the feeding program in schools in Nyeri District. The comparative monthly figure in Kiambu District for 1995 was around Kenya Shillings 250 per month. These figures give an impression of a cheap program, and while this may be the case, two points need to be borne in mind. First is the high dependency of the program on Government and donor support which begs the question about its sustainability. Second is the low-involvement in the program of poor parents which seems to indicate that some hidden costs make the program more expensive than it appears and this situation raises serious questions about the initial objectives of the program.

Initiatives Offering School Facilities and Resources

Background and Rationale

Evidence from many less industrialized countries supports a positive relationship between student achievement and availability of such key learning resources as textbooks, good classrooms, desks and chairs. Textbooks in particular are an important input in the learning process. Unfortunately, in many African schools such resources are often lacking.

In Kenya there exists a severe problem of paucity of learning resources in primary schools. In fact, the implementation of the 8-4-4 curriculum in 1985, exacerbated an already bad situation. In many of the rural and urban schools the construction of a classrooms and workshops to accommodate extra classes following extension of the primary cycle by one year, was not completed, and where they were, the resources such as desks, chairs and tool kits were unavailable.

There are a number of organizations and groups which provide school facilities and resources to children in primary schools particularly in poor nomadic districts and urban slums. Six initiatives in this kind of activity were studied. They were Action Aid of Kenya working in an urban slum called Kariobangi in the eastern part of Nairobi; Christian Children Fund project in five administrative divisions of Samburu district in northern Kenya; Wamba Community Project also in Samburu district; Plan International and Compassion International in Embu district about 100 miles northeast of Nairobi; and Stephen Kanja Primary School project in Majimboni, Kwale district south of Mombassa.

Action Aid Kenya has been operating in the country since 1974. In 1995, Action Aid supported integrated development programs in six designated areas each with a population approximating 60,000. Only one of the six areas, Action Aid Kariobange was in an urban area. This urban program is located in the slums of Kariobangi and Korogocho, covering an area of about 10 square kilometers.

The Kariobangi program was started in 1987 through funding by the Catholic Church Kariobangi, Nairobi, in a slum area characterized by poverty and unemployment. The program provides for school facilities and learning materials. It was started through the efforts of the headmaster of Baba Dogo primary school who approached donors and explained the dilemma of school children who hail from slums. A survey conducted by Action Aid showed the need for intervention. After conducting a survey, Action Aid started a program of assisting children enrolled in four slum schools Korogocho, Marura, Nguyumu and Baba Doga which fall within the jurisdiction of Kariobangi project. Although generally all community members resident in the areas of Action Aid operations benefit in one way or another, the focus is largely on children of poor single women. In addition to a Spain based Child Sponsorship Scheme, there are other organizations which collaborate with Action Aid in the provision of school facilities and resources. These include the Catholic Church which runs school feeding programs; Redeemed Church which provides school fees and uniforms to some needy children; World Vision and Child Care International which gives scholarships and school uniforms; and, the Nairobi City Council which promotes de-worming campaigns in schools.

The second program scrutinized under School Facilities and Resources initiative is Compassion International in Embu, which started operating in 1984 through the Bishop of the Church of the Province of Kenya. The organization operates in Gachoka Division which is drought stricken with many families who are unable economically to support themselves. As a result, there were many children who could not go to school due to lack of funds to pay fees and other educational levies. Upon receiving requests for help, the Bishop contacted Compassion International which agreed to start development initiatives in Embu district where it works in collaboration with the Church of the Province of Kenya (CPK). The project focusses on the purchase of textbooks, exercise books, teaching materials, desks, uniforms for the sponsored children, health care and the construction water tanks.

The intended beneficiaries of this program are children from poor families who need assistance to acquire necessary learning resources, facilities and equipment. Some poor parents also receive support to start income generating activities as a way out of their impoverished condition.

The third program surveyed was Plan International which, like Compassion International, was operating in Embu District. Plan International started its services in Embu District in 1982 after being invited there by an influential member of parliament who was responding to a request for financial assistance from parents in both Gachoka and Siakago divisions of the district.

Plan International-Embu is sponsored by Plan International which has its headquarters in the U.S.A. When it started its operations, Plan International's main focus was the sponsorship of individual children. Later, their scope of activities covered entire community with the provision of health, water and sanitation and other essential services. The organization also supplies selected schools with learning and teaching facilities and resources through much of Gachoka and Siakago divisions with the intended beneficiaries being all children in the client schools.

The fourth program evaluated under the provision of school facilities and resources initiative was Christian Children Fund (CCF) whose operations were in the arid Samburu District in the northern part of the vast Rift Valley Province. Samburu District is predominantly arid and therefore unfavorable for agricultural activities except for the keeping of some domestic livestock. Prolonged droughts are common and these decimate livestock and lead to famine. Pastoralism is the major way of life in this district.

It was in fact after a serious drought that in 1974 Catholic Church in Samburu initiated a program of support to some families to enable them to educate their children. The CCF was subsequently invited to support and expand this program of assistance to families for children's education. The Catholic Church in Samburu was of the view that CCF's support would ensure an expanded and sustainable program. The Catholic Church formally handed over the assistance program CCF in 1986. This organization has its Kenyan head office in the city of Nairobi.

Most of the children supported by the CCF are of Samburu and Turkana ethnic origin, the two dominant ethnic communities in Samburu District. Only needy children enrolled in pre-school and primary schools have been the intended beneficiaries of this program.

Another intervention covered by the evaluation study was Wamba Community project. The project, located in Wamba Division of Samburu District, was started by World Vision in 1982 in response to household hardships a series of devastating droughts at the start of the 1980s. The initiative was started as a community development project with a focus on selective support for a specific school and direct sponsorship for individual children. When World Vision realized that it was getting difficult to attain set goals and ensure sustainability without the participation of the local community members, it expanded the project in 1989 to incorporate them. With this changed focus, most community members including pupils, parents and teachers started to benefit from the initiative.

The last program studied under the school facilities and resources initiative was Stephen Kanja (Majimboni) Primary School. The school is located in Majimboni location within Shimba Hills educational zone in Kwale District, Coast Province, the south-eastern part of Kenya. The school was started in 1965 two years after the country became independent from colonial rule, and was officially known as Majimboni Primary School.

Like may other schools in Kwale District, Majimboni Primary School had very modest physical facilities and learning resources which were deteriorating with each passing year. It happened that one day in 1985 a tour guide Stephen Kanja in one of his journeys between Mombassa and Shimba Hills National Park, visited this Majimboni Primary School during a heavy rainfall. He noticed that some lessons were interrupted because pupils took them under trees while in other classrooms pupils could not concentrate on learning because of leaking roofs. Mr. Stephen Kanja was visibly moved by this pathetic situation and subsequently requested a group of philanthropic tourists to assist in building and rehabilitating the school. Response was swift and positive, and the fact the school lies beside the main tourist route linking Mombassa to the Shimba Hills National Park proved and continues to prove strategic.

It was in recognition of the important role played by Mr Kanja in getting Majimboni Primary School rehabilitated that school authorities had its name changed to Stephen Kanja Primary School. Beneficiaries include pre-school and primary school children as well as their parents and teachers.

Objectives and Organizational Structure

Programs devoted to the provision of school resources and facilities that were examined in this study shared a number of objectives. This is not surprising since they essentially undertook to offer similar services. In a few instances some programs offered additional objectives depending on the history of the initiative or the peculiar circumstances of its clients. The six programs under the School Facilities and Resources Initiative shared three central objectives as follows: a) To uplift the right of the child and family through the provision of education, health care and sanitation; b) To help children from poor families to attend school through the provision of school fees, uniforms, textbooks and other related resources; c) To promote education of poor children through the construction of physical facilities in schools and ensure their supply with desks and chairs for pupils.

The three objectives specified above form the core activities of this type of initiative. In fact, the first objective outlined above is a broad one that gives shape to the second and third. All three objectives take account of children in the social context of the family and or the community. In this sense, support provided to the child must in some respects be extended to the family or the community.

Some other objectives of the programs incorporated under school facilities and resources initiative were specific to one or two of these programs. For example one objective was shared by Action Aid and Plan International. The shared objective is; to economically empower parents in those communities in which the initiative operates.

This objective was seen as an answer to the amelioration of the syndrome of poverty many households found themselves trapped in. Economic empowerment of parents would enable the parents to acquire the requisite resources for the education and rearing of their children and would thus render donor aid unnecessary.

Action Aid, and Wamba Community Project sponsored by World Vision, shared two objectives namely; to improve the health status of school children through the provision of school lunch programs, to facilitate the provision of piped (clean) water to communities and schools. Availability of lunch and clean water for children, particularly those enrolled in school, was regarded as an important aspect of the two programs.

In addition two objectives each were articulated uniquely by CCF on the one hand and Stephen Kanja primary school initiative on the other hand. Thus, CCF further intended to create employment opportunities for school leavers through job training and to organize sponsor-relations day when community is sensitized on what role is expected of all beneficiaries.

Many of the programs focusing largely on the provision of school facilities and resources for children in pre-school and primary school hardly bothered with such issues as post-school training. Their main concern was to assist children complete primary school education. Paying some attention, no matter how minor to the post-school training of some of the children was unique objective of CCF. The Stephen Kanja primary school program had the following two additional objectives; to promote pre-school education in the area around the school, and to help the school attain self-reliance in the event that sponsorship ends.

The objective on pre-school education was meant to assist the school recruit a large number of children and who would easily cope with primary school education. This was an important strategy in Kwale district where many families resist enrolling children in secular schools out of fear that such exposure may undermine Islamic Koranic education.

The other objective on ultimate self-reliance for the Stephen Kanja primary school initiative is one that concerns all aid assisted programs. Unlike Stepehen Kanja primary school experiment, many aid assisted programs are normally silent about this very important objective. As a result of lack of focus on this objective, many foreign sponsored programs face an uncertain future when confronted with termination of sponsorship.

Finally, Action Aid program in Kariobangi had one objective focused on the quality of primary education in those schools under its sponsorship. This objective focused on; improvement of education in schools by several strategies including training of teachers and lay members of the parents-teachers association (PTA).

Among all the six programs devoted to the provision of school facilities and resources, only Action Aid, Kariobangi, allocated resources for in-service training of teachers and committee members of the PTA, particularly in the issue of school management. The training of school committee members is key aspects of school management was seen by Action Aid as an important strategy in empowering parents as stakeholders to have some control in the affairs of the school.

The way the six programs which fall under the school facilities and resources initiative are organized for administrative purposes is a point we turn to here. Four of the six programs namely Action Aid, Compassion International, Plan International and Wamba Community project which is sponsored by World Vision, have quite similar administrative structures. These organizations which sponsor the different programs have headquarters office in Nairobi. In their areas of operation, each has a field office headed by an executive manager or a project manager with one or two deputy managers. These officials are the key representatives of the donor organization in the communities which are serviced.

Assisting each group of donor representatives in running the program is a management committee consisting of representatives of key stakeholders such as other program staff members, religious organizations and parents-teachers associations. The management committee serving each of the four programs ensures that needs of school children, their parents and other members of the community are identified, deliberated upon and forwarded to the headquarters of the program in Nairobi for funding. For Action Aid's Kariobangi Program, Compassion International and the Plan International both in Embu district, management committees are specific parents-teachers association (PTA) committees in each client school. The representatives of the sponsoring body are social workers located within the school compound. These PTA committees are run more democratically than other forms of administrative arrangements. The cases of Christian Children Fund (CCF) and Stephen Kanja primary school clearly demonstrate this. The administrative structure of Wamba Community project falls somewhere between the two extremes represented by the first four and the second two programs mentioned above.

The Wamba Community Project management committee does not have representatives on the PTAs of schools served by the project but has representatives of the larger community within which schools are located. What makes the membership of the committee undemocratic is the selection of community representatives through proposals by church leaders and members of the local administration such as chiefs and assistant chiefs. There is nothing to prevent these grassroots leaders from proposing incompetent relatives or friends to serve in the management committees, especially given that those community representatives receive some allowances.

It was within the Christian Children Fund (CCF) program and that of Stephen Kanja Primary School, that the management structure had a strong undemocratic element. The CCF program in Samburu District has a field office in Embu town, complete with a project manager. The management committee which assists the project manager has representatives of schools and parents. Articulation of the concerns of teachers, parents and pupils is therefore, not effectively done. In the case of Stephen Kanja Primary School program, a strong committee of the PTA exists but only a loose committee of the donors. The links between the PTA committee and the donor's committee are sporadic and unequal. Often the donors have carried out activities without full consultation with members of the school PTA committee. This practice, when it does occur, is of course undemocratic.

Initiative's Activities and Services

The initiatives on school facilities and resources provide resources for education directly. They also provide other services which in one way or another support the education of children. Among the basic services offered by this kind of initiative are: a) construction of classrooms and workshops for schools and toilets, boreholes and water tanks for both schools and communities; b) the provision of desks and chairs for pupils and furniture for staff rooms; c)the provision of textbooks, other learning materials and teaching aids; d) support with school uniforms and fees for selected pupils; e) support for school feeding programs; f) assistance to co-curricular activities in the form of meeting transport and accommodation costs.

The above six activities provide relief to parents and pupils who are unable to meet costs which would arise if someone else had not provided them. As such, one would expect that in meeting these costs, the programs further the objective of giving access to primary education for children from poor households.

In addition to the above six shared activities, some of the initiatives gave additional services. For instance both Plan International and CCF also offered health services in the form of sanitation and immunization and the provision of drugs and mosquito nets at affordable prices. Both CCF and Action Aid made available, for some community members, soft loans to promote small scale enterprises. This was done as an attempt to break the circle of poverty which made parents unable to support the costs of their children's education. Action Aid and Plan International train members of the local community, the former focusing on teachers and lay members of school PTAs in school management, and the latter on community adults about health improvement. Additionally, Stephen Kanja primary school project has initiated a pre-school program for children in the vicinity of the primary school. In this way, the school ensures it has an adequate supply of quality candidates for grade/standard one each year.

In undertaking the various activities, the sponsors of the programs expect members of the communities to make a contribution. Such contributions usually take the form of free labor and supply of some building materials. The contributions of members of the community may not easily be quantified in monetary terms. But are nonetheless substantial. In the case of Plan International it is in fact the responsibility of the community to pay the contractor's labor costs.

Table 7.2   Costs of Operating Aspects of Wamba and Kanja Initiatives (1995)

A. WAMBA PROJECT		B. STEPHAN KANJA PROJECT	
Activity line	Cost in Million Kenya Shillings	Activity Line	Cost in Million Kenya Shillings
Primary education	1.0	Construction of administration block	0.8
Post primary education and training	1.5	Construction of workshop/home Science room	0.8
Other projects	2.5	Construction of classrooms	0.72
Total	5.0	Total	2.32

A point made earlier about difficulties in obtaining information on the costs of programs applies in the case of initiatives providing School Facilities and Resources. Where information was obtained on costs, it was extremely sketchy. Only two of the six programs under this initiative provided information on costs that gives an indication of the levels of funds involved. (See Table 7.2)

Initiatives on Non-formal Education

Background and Rationale

Although considerable expansion in enrolment in formal education has taken place at all levels in Kenya since the country gained political independence in 1963, many children of school-going age are still left out of the educational system. Those most affected by this exclusion are children from poor families, particularly in rural and arid or semi arid areas and urban slums. Thus while gross national enrolment ratio in primary school education was around 85 per cent in 1995, the ratio was only between 20 and 24 per cent in the arid and semi-arid in Eastern and North Eastern Provinces.

Some of the children who are unable to join or continue with mainstream formal primary schools manage to get into alternative educational programs for purposes of acquiring literacy and training. These alternative educational programs are what we refer to in this study as non-formal education initiatives.

Non-formal education is regarded here as an organized, systematic, educational activity carried outside the formal educational system. In Kenya these programs are alternative schools to the formal system and cater mainly for economically and socially disadvantaged children.

The Non-formal Education initiatives studied were eight. Two of them: Nadirkonyen Catholic Street Children Center and Bendera (Baragoi) Out of School Center are located in ASAL regions of Turkana and Samburu Districts respectively. The former center is located in Lodwar town, and the latter is in Baragoi town. Four of the initiatives: Jamaa Home, St. John's Community and Undugu Center are located in different low status residential areas of Nairobi, in the Eastlands region of the city. Jamaa Home and St. John's Community are located in Uhuru and Pumwani Estates respectively, while the Undugu Society programs we visited are in Shaurimoyo Estate, overlooking Muthurwa Railway quarters (there are several Undugu Society programs in the city). Pandpieri and Kisumu Evening continuation classes are located in Kisumu District in Nyanza Province of Kenya. The former is situated in Nyalenda Estate in the Eastern section of Kisumu town, Kenya's third largest city. The continuation classes program is spread out of several centers in Kisumu town and rural Kisumu District. Wema Center is located in the Likoni area in Mombassa, Kenya's second largest city.

The Undugu Center was started in 1975 by a Catholic priest Father Grol, in reaction to the problem of street children. Initially the focus of the Center was on boys only; later street girls were also included. The Undugu Basic Education Program in Pumwani Estate, Nairobi, was launched in 1979. Its focus was to provide basic education and skills training to street children who had missed the opportunity to receive education in the formal school program. The Undugu society that runs the basic education program is sponsored by catholic organizations in Kenya and by a number of German and Dutch organizations.

The second program studied under non-formal education was St. John's Community. The Community was started in 1956 in the Pumwani slum area by the Church Missionary Society (CMS) under the directorship of Ms. Anne Barnett. Initially its main function was the provision of literacy and numeracy to adults. Later, particularly after Kenya's political independence in 1963, parents convinced St. John's Community to give their children, rather than themselves the opportunity to acquire an education. The community accepted this request and currently it offers basic education and skill training to children not catered for by the formal education system. Its basic education program is structured along lines similar to the formal education system which has in fact allowed some children from St. John's basic education offering to be channeled to formal primary and secondary schools. The Church of the Province of Kenya (Anglican) and, a number of overseas organization are the major funders of the St. John's Community.

Jamaa Home, the third non-formal education initiative studied in the City of Nairobi, was started by the Catholic Lady of Charity Sisters in the late 1960s to cater for young girls who became pregnant while in school. The Lady of Charity Sisters initially started a maternity hospital called Jamaa,in Uhuru Estate in the eastern part of the City of Nairobi. When the home for pregnant school girls was started, it was housed within the Jamaa Maternity Hospital. The main idea behind Jamaa Home is the rehabilitation of pregnant girls so that they are reintegrated within their families and, for those who so desire, re-routed back to formal schools to continue their education. Sponsors of the program include the Catholic church, the National Council of Churches of Kenya, Redeemed Church, American Women's Organization and individuals within and outside Kenya.

The non-formal education program known as the Kisumu Evening Continuation Classes has a checkered history. It started slowly in 1968 with some six adults who were keen to receive literacy and numeracy and who were supported by the then Director of Social Services Kisusmu Municipality. Starting in 1969, the University College, Nairobi, took over the program and enrolment increased quickly over the years. One unique aspect of this program has been its ability to attract girls and boys who work during the day as domestic help (ayas in Kiswahili) but are able to attend the evening classes. The majority of the learners however, are young adults who dropped out of the formal education system.

There are two components to this program. First is the evening continuation classes located in Kisumu town at Arina, Kaloleni Union and Kisumu Central centers and sponsored by the Kisumu Municipal Council. Second is Kisumu rural evening classes located in Kamdhira and Awasi which were started in 1994 by the Department of Adult Education in the Ministry of Culture and Social Services. Apart from these institutions, other sponsors are the Ministry of Education and UNICEF. Members of the community offer support by providing buildings for the classes and money for buying some learning materials.

Pandpieri Street Children's Program, also in Kisumu Municipality, was started in the late 1970s by a Catholic priest initially to provide recreation activities for street children. In 1980, the Pandpieri Catholic Center opened its doors to street children. When the number of children became quite large, the program became more structured and adopted children's rehabilitation as its main focus. The rehabilitation includes provision of literacy, skills training, and counseling. The Catholic Center, Nyalenda Home and Bala Halfway House are sponsored by UNICEF, Caritas Sisters (a Catholic Organization of Holland) and Catholic Church in Kenya.

The sixth and seventh non-formal education programs investigated were, Nadirkonyen Catholic Street Children Center and Bendera (Baragoi) out of School Youth Program, solely serve rural children in two pastoralist districts of arid northern Kenya. As mentioned earlier, Nadirkonyen Center is in Lodwar Town, Turkana District, while Bandera program is in Baragoi Town, Samburu District. Both districts are characterized by frequent droughts, food shortage and low enrolment in primary school education.

The Nadirkonyen Center was started in Lodwar town in 1991 by the Catholic Diocese of Lodwar to cater for poor and hungry street children. In starting the Center, the sponsor hoped to rehabilitate the children and assist them to continue with their education.

The Bendera Out of School Youth Program in Baragoi town was started in 1990 by a local politician who was reacting to a rising wave of idle, uneducated youth whose animal herds had been wiped out by drought. The local politician, Councillor Alloys Letpila, felt that something positive needed to be done to prevent the displaced youth from becoming antisocial menace. He started the out of school youth program as an evening playgroup organization for children in Manyattas (local homesteads) around Baragoi town. The playgroup organization started in a Center that already had an on-going nursery school.

By 1991, the playgroup program evolved into an evening class for English, Kiswahili and Mathematics. Within 1992, all subjects taught in the formal primary school system were introduced as part of the evening youth classes. In January 1993, a formal primary school was established at the center to absorb children from the nursery school and to assist the subject offerings through evening and night classes. These are particularly popular with many youth because they attend them after completing household chores such as herding and fetching water and firewood. The Bendera out of school Youth program is sponsored by the local Catholic Church, the Christian Children Fund (CCF) German Agency for International Cooperation (GTZ), Samburu District Development Committee and parents. The Kenya Institute of Education, an organ of the Ministry of Education guides the programs's primary education curriculum.

The final non-formal education initiative considered in the evaluation study was the City of Mombassa based Wema Center. It was started in 1993 by a pioneer woman Mrs. Yinda, whose backgrounds as a sociologist and a mother motivated her to establish a Center to rehabilitate street girls. The Wema Center of which she is the Director provides shelter, education and health services for the destitute street girls. The non-formal education program at the Center offers regular primary school subjects in a setting that is not a formal school. The Wema Center is sponsored by its Director, the Child Welfare Society of Kenya, International Labor Organization (ILO), UNICEF and private individuals. The mentioned organizations are sponsors in the sense that they contribute funds, however modest, to support some of center's activities.

Objectives and Organizational Structure

Given the kinds of children and youth many of the non-formal education initiatives serve and the circumstances of these children, it is perhaps not surprising that the initiatives have remarkably similar objectives. Emphasis in objectives may vary from one initiative to the next, but the basic objectives are the same.

Some twelve objectives cut across virtually all of the eight non-formal education programs that were evaluated. There were a few objectives that seemed specific to certain objectives and we shall mention them shortly. The eight non-formal education initiatives shared the following objectives: a) To rehabilitate and facilitate the development of disadvantaged who did not attend formal education and reroute some of them, especially girls, to formal education programs; b) To establish learning Centers and institutions for disadvantaged youth and equip them with knowledge and skills for self-reliance; c) To enable youth who are unable to fit in the inflexible formal education system to get education under a different arrangement; d) To assist disadvantaged children acquire skills in basic education in formal schools; e) To arouse interest in education so that some pupils from non-formal education programs can filter to the regular schools; f) To support and sponsor disadvantaged youth in formal learning institutions; g) To reduce illiteracy by promoting access to education through non-formal channels; h) To assist pupils develop confidence and positively interact with others; i) To identify and attach disadvantaged youth to relevant artisan training in order for them to acquire practical skills for self-employment; j) To mobilize and empower marginalized individuals, groups and communities for sustainable community development; k) To study or research, document and initiate innovative development activities in response to emerging poverty issues; l) To solicit support and procure human and non human resources in order to support the activities of the program.

Three themes run through the outlined objectives. First, the programs targeted children out of the formal school system. Many of these were from deprived social backgrounds. Second these children primarily receive educational packages for gaining literacy and arithmetical skills. In this provision of education, non-formal channels were given priority but there always was concern that formal education curriculum serve as the yardstick. Transfers across the two forms of education were accepted by the managers of the non-formal education programs and some managers of the formal education programs and some managers of the formal education system.

Third, many of the non-formal education initiatives had a training component for acquisition of practical skills for salaried employment or self-employment. These were to be sure ambitious objectives but in sticking to and working towards them, the non-formal education programs filled a much felt gap.

As mentioned in a previous paragraph of this subsection, there were a few objectives that were specific to certain initiatives. Thus, Undugu Basic Education Program had three additional goals namely, a) to develop a continuing assessment plan of the disadvantaged individuals, groups and communities; b) to identify successful individuals or groups formerly supported and encourage them to subscribe to Undugu mission; and c) to network and support groups, individuals and organizations with similar interests and pursuits as Undugu Society. These three broad objectives were probably implicit in the thinking of the other seven programs; at best there was no clause in any of the objectives of the seven other initiatives that contradicted or opposed these three from Undugu Society.

Bendera and Nadirkonyen programs had one additional goal each. For the former it was to give the herds boys and herds girls a second chance of getting education while attending to their traditional duties. The idea here is that the Bendera out of school youth program accommodated the nomadic lifestyle of the learners in allowing them to attend non-formal classes in the evening and at night after attending to such chores as looking after livestock, collecting firewood and water. For the latter program, Nadirkonyen, the extra objective was to stop the migration of street children from Turkana towns to outside districts.

We turn next to organizational structure of the eight non-formal education initiatives. Five of the eight programs, Undugu, Jamaa, Pandpieri, Nadirkonyen and Bendera, have strong ties to Catholic Church in the area of the program operation. This church serves as the head office of the five programs and is delegated to a team of personnel without any noticeable interference from the catholic diocesan office.

The administrative head of each of the five church-supported programs is the program Coordinator or Center Coordinator or, in the case of Jamaa Home the Sister Superior. There may be an assistant to take care of the business in the absence of the Coordinator. These assistants were often teachers and social workers. The former focus on the instructional function of the program and the latter focus on support services for the children, youth or pupils. Only the Bendera out of school Youth Program did not have social workers, perhaps because most of the clients it caters for are non-problem children from nearby families.

It is a weakness in the administrative set up of the five programs that the community within which each functions is not formally represented. It is true that they are usually consulted on critical issues, but they do not have direct representation in the decision making process of the program.

Of the remaining three non-formal education programs, Kisumu Evening Continuation classes and St. John's Community, have a deeper administrative structure than Wema Center. The Kisumu programs, has a dual head-office, one being within the Municipal Education Office and other in the District Adult Education Office. In running the Evening Continuation Classes these two offices consult not only with each other, but also with the District Education Office which is concerned with the formal education system. The guidance of this last office is required since the Evening Continuation Classes follow the curriculum of the formal education system. As one can readily anticipate, these administrative arrangements are bound to at times lead to confusion, especially for subordinate staff. These subordinate staff in the management of the programs are teachers and representatives of communities in which learning Centers are located.

The administrative arrangement of St. John's Community is somewhat simpler than that of the Kisumu Evening Continuation Classes. Policy matters of the St. John's Community are handled by a Board of Directors. The day-by-day activities are the responsibility of the Manager. Below the Manager is the Head Teacher for non-formal education program. The Head Teacher consults with the manager on all matters related to non-formal education activities. Supporting the Head Teacher are a team of teachers who handle instruction and one or two social workers who attend to the non-instructional needs of the learners.

The organizational structure of Wema Center simply consists of the Director who is the founder, and a few teachers, a matron who pays attention to the health issues and hostel workers who look after the girls' general welfare.

In summary, the organizational structure of the non-formal educational programs are simple with clear line authority which facilitates consultation among management staff. The exception is the Kisumu Evening Continuation Class where the line of authority is ambiguous. Yet it is this last program that has made a provision for the community to be represented in the decision making structure of the program. The others have not officially done this thereby assuming a patronizing orientation.

The point has been made that the primary objective of the non-formal education initiative is the provision of education, literacy and skills training for mainly disadvantaged children who for one reason or another missed out on the formal education system. The question here is what activities and services do programs under this initiatives undertake in pursuit of the goals that have been stipulated.

To start with, the tasks the programs undertakes in pursuit of their objectives are by and large similar. There may be differences in emphasis in the performance of some tasks, but there are hardly instances where basic tasks are ignored by a program.

Second, the basic tasks undertaken by the programs included: a) Enrolment and teaching of children in literacy and numeracy skills. The tendency was to follow the curriculum of formal schools underwritten by the Kenya Institute of Education (KIE); b) Implementation of training programs in carpentry, metal work, tailoring and secretarial skills. Learners were freely provided with machinery and materials; c) The provision of rehabilitation services which included counseling, socialization, recreation sports and religious education. The idea was to change the behavior of street children to acceptable social norms; d) Recruitment of children from the streets, which often entailed assisting them, while still in the street, with food, clothing and medicines; e) Provision of books and other learning materials for sponsored children; f) Sponsorship of children for education, in some cases at the university level; g) Re-routing of some children in non-formal education to the formal education system; h) Attention to health care for the children through provision of adequate food and medicines; i) Re-routing of some street children to their families after successful rehabilitation and education at the centers.

It is important, along lines of gender, to emphasize that Jamaa Home and Wema Center were the two programs that focused exclusively on girls. In this respect, their activities benefitted girls. Pregnant girls and young mothers received shelter, food, medicine and guidance and counseling at these two centers. The number of street girls is growing and may in the near future catch up with that of boys, hence there is need for more programs such as Jamaa and Wema Center to cater for girls in especially difficult circumstances.

Table 7.3 Annual Costs Associated with Three Non-formal Education Programs

A. Undugu Society (1993)	
Activity Line	Cost in Million Kenya Shillings
Social services	10.000
Salaries and Administration	12.000
School sponsorship	4.000
Basic Education	4.000
Schools	4.000
Vehicles and fuel	50.000
Total	80.000

B. Wemba Center (1995)	
Rent	·0.180
Water	0.180
Electricity	0.252
School Sponsorship	0.084
Salaries	0.240
Food and others	0.550
Total	1.486

C. Nadirkonyen Center (1995)	
Education sector	0.200
Salaries	0.160
Transport	0.155
Health	0.036
Clothes	0.060
Equipment	0.036
Food and others	0.353
Total	1.000

Appreciable information on costs was obtained for three programs among the non-formal education initiatives. Table 7.3 carries the information.

The figures in Table 7.3 suggest that Undugu society, which is much older and more diversified in its programs than either Wema Center or Nadirkonyen Programs, had a much larger budgetary outlay. In 1993, the program had to purchase a number of vehicles, which in fact pushed its operational costs up very markedly. It should be noted that the direct costs of running the basic education schools was only around 4 million shillings.

The costs of running Wema Center and the Nadirkonyen Youth Program were about the same. Food and other items were in both cases the most expensive. Since in both cases the figures were provided by the Directors as approximate costs, it is probably the case that the centers are much more expensive to run than the figures would suggest. It is to be expected that the general orientation of many program senior staff is to under report income and, by implication, expense figures in the centers, perhaps to make the point that their programs are merely surviving and can make do with more financial contributions.

Community Initiatives

Background and Rationale

In the evaluation study that was undertaken, community initiatives were those started by members of a community. They were started on the basis of the principles of felt needs, agreed upon goals and co-operation. This means that most of the members of the community look at the initiatives as belonging to them. In addition, most of the community members were fully involved in planning and implementing the initiatives' activities.

Most of the community initiatives reported in this section were initiated by the respective communities. Members of the community felt the need and came up with the idea of starting the initiative to address their problems. In a few cases, the initiatives were started by a few members who subsequently sensitized the rest of the community about the benefits of the initiative. Although a community may receive some assistance from donor or the government, the community members remain the owner of the initiative. As owners they are involved in planning, implementing, monitoring and evaluation of the activities of the initiative. Most of the initiatives basically targeted the education of children from poor families in the community as well as ensured that as many children as possible enroll and remain in school until they complete the primary school cycle.

Six community initiatives were studied namely; Madrassa Resource Center Kongowea Community Schools, Inuka Self Help Nursery and Primary School, Muhaka Islamic Center, Waa Primary School and the Islamic Al-Noor Nursery Schools. Both Madrasa Resource Center and Kongowea community school are located on the main island of Mombassa town at the Kenyan coast. Inuka Self Help and Primary School is located in Likoni Division of Mombassa District. Two initiatives namely Muhaka Islamic Center and Waa Primary School are in Kwale District south of Mombassa. The final initiative evaluated is the Islamic Al-Noor Nursery and primary school located in Lodwar town in Turkana District, northern Kenya.

The Aga Khan Foundation carried out a study which led to the establishment of Madrasa Resource Center in 1986 to develop participatory community based model of pre-school education with Islamic religious traditions and culture. Islamic children were unable to attend secular education because their parents feared that western education would alienate them from an Islamic way of life. There was need for an approach which would integrate both Islamic and secular education. It was through the establishment of the Madrassa Resource Center that the Aga Khan Foundation was able to launch an integrated curriculum designed to prepare Muslim children for primary education by enhancing their access to schooling. In addition it was to enhance their chances of performing well in secular schools while at the same time maintaining Islamic religious instruction.

Kongowea initiatives was started by the community with the assistance of the Ministry of Culture and Social Services. It was to cater for the educational needs of poor children who had either dropped out of school or had never enrolled due to the parents' inability to meet the financial requirements of the secular primary school. It was set up in 1994 to meet the educational needs of children from Kongowea Estate and the neighboring communities who were unable for one reason or another to participate in the formal education system.

Inuka Self Help and Primary school situated in Likoni division of Mombassa District was set up around 1988 by a group of three doctors. The doctors had noticed that most of the parents from this slum area were unable to pay enrolment levies in secular primary schools to enable their children to gain access to schooling. School attendance was also low due to negative attitudes towards girls' education, early marriages and pregnancies. The doctors started the Inuka educational program to improve the participation of the local children in schooling. The doctors also intended to provide medical services to the local community and therefore built a small hospital in the vicinity of the school.

Muhaka Islamic Center, situated in Diani location of Kwale District, was set up by the local community based on the need for an integrated curriculum. The notion of an integrated curriculum was sold to the community by Muslim teacher (Maalim) who was the principal of the Center and the community embraced the idea. The nursery school follows an integrated curriculum where both secular and Islamic religious education are taught. The primary school follows the official 8-4-4 curriculum of the Ministry of Education but integrates it with some Islamic teaching.

Waa Primary School in Ngombeni Waa zone in Kwale is an old institution. The low-cost boarding section for girls was started by the Kwale County Council in 1960; when it was realized that many school girls became pregnant or entered early marriages. It was thought that restriction in boarding school would curtail some of these problems. Initially the Kwale County Council met the financial cost of the boarding section for girls. In 1992, however, parents were asked to enter into a cost sharing arrangement with the Government and the Kwale County Council. Since that time the parents shoulder the direct costs of running the boarding section for girls except for the salaries of the school matron and cooks who are paid by the Kwale County Council, and teacher's salaries which come from the Kenyan Government.

The Islamic Al-Noor Nursery and primary School in Lodwar town in Turkana District was set up by the Muslim Community and was intended to benefit the homeless and destitute local Turkana children through the provision of educational and facilities and resources. Another need was to induct the supported children into the Islamic religion and way of life. The initiative is funded by the Islamic community through the Jamia Mosque of Nairobi and the Islamic Foundation of the Young Muslim League.

Objectives and Organizational Structure

In outlining and discussing the aims of the six community initiatives that were studied, it is important to bear in mind that these initiatives fell into broad types: those sponsored under the tutelage of Islamic organization or groups;

and those sponsored by communities as part of secular institutions. Belonging in the first category are Madrassa Resource Center Al-Noor Nursery and primary School and Muhaka Islamic Center. In the second category are the remaining three initiatives namely Kongowea Community School, Inuka Self-help Nursery School and Waa Primary School. The objectives of the initiatives reflect this difference in the orientations of the founders.

The three initiatives which were overtly influenced by Islamic values have the following objectives: a) To create awareness about secular education and make the community appreciate this type of education as they do Islamic Education; b) To promote integrated curriculum that focuses on both Islamic way of life and secular education; c) To help children of Moslem backgrounds get Islamic and secular education at the same time and thereby reduce the learning period; d) To combine secular and Islamic education and thus reduce the expense on education; e) To develop teaching aids appropriate to Islamic children that address the objective of enhancing Islamic religious and secular education; f) To offer in-service training opportunities for pre-school teachers from schools under the management of the Madrassa Resource Center; g) To improve the education standards of Islamic children by increasing school enrolment, retention and performance.

The outlined seven objectives underscore the concern to harmonize Islamic and Secular education. The urgency about getting Muslim communities to accommodate secular education in increasing numbers was announced by founders of the three initiatives out of an awareness that Muslims were in the years after independence increasingly bypassed in allocation to important role in Kenyan society and largely on account of their low educational attainment. The objectives mentioned in the foregoing section make it clear that some Moslem activists felt the need for this undesirable cycle to be broken.

We shift attention to the objectives of the remaining three community initiatives that we have pointed out were largely secular in nature. Inuka and Waa were essentially formal education initiatives. The former took the form of a private school, what in Kenyan nomenclature would be called an harambee (self-help) school, that offered pre-school and primary school education. The latter was an old primary school. Under the initiative a boarding section was set up for girls and was supported with resources from within the community.

The two initiatives therefore shared the following familiar formal objective; to provide pre-school and primary school education to children in the neighboring communities. Outside the shared objective, the Inuka initiative had this unique objective; to improve the education and health standards of the community around the school through support for the children. This objective was central to starting the initiative since children of poor parents that failed to enroll and remain in school would now be admitted either through sponsorship or at very minimal cost to parents or guardians. Moreover, the doctors who established the initiative built a health facility that was to cater for the health needs of the same children. At least these were the expectations related to the initiatives when they were implemented.

Waa Primary school initiative for girls, had two objectives that were partial to this section of the school preparation. In effect, the initiative intended to achieve the following two objectives: a) To give girls a conclusive atmosphere to study; b) To offer female pupils adequate counseling and to prevent unwanted sexual activities in order to avoid unwanted pregnancies and premature (child) marriages.

At least the initiative raised points which have often been advanced in rationalizing the need for boarding schools for girls, especially in areas at a higher risk of failing to enroll and stay in school because of parental apathy towards their education or the practice of marrying them off early.

Lastly, Kongowea Community initiative was conceived as an alternative school to formal education for children who were unable to attend the latter. In this respect, it is similar to a non-formal education initiative, but one which is started and managed by members of the community themselves. Its objectives echo some of those on non-formal education as the following two objectives make clear: a) To promote literacy and numeracy among the children and youth from poor parents in the catchment areas of the program; b) To assist in rehabilitating street children by removing them from the streets and helping them to have access to education cheaply.

The two objectives are self-explanatory and what will need explaining is the extent to which they have been pursued and with what results. A close examination reveals that the three initiatives under strong sponsorship of Islamic group reflect this fact in their administrative arrangement. Thus, the Madrassa Resource Center, Al-Noor Nursery and primary school and Muhaka Islamic Center, are all managed by Islamic Executive Committees. In the Madrassa Resource Center case, this executive committee has a strong presence of the Aga Khan Foundation. In the case of the Al-Noor Nursery and Primary School program, the executive committee is under the Jamia Mosque which is the major sponsor. The important management body for Muhaka Islamic Center is a committee of Muslim parents from the neighboring community. These executive committees are the policy organs of the mentioned community initiatives.

Day to day management of the three programs is headed by a Center Manager or Director. These are individuals of strong Islamic faith and they ensure that the programs uphold the Islamic way of life. The Madrassa Resource Center has a dual and slightly deeper hierarchy than either Muhaka Islamic Center or the Al-Noor Nursery and Primary School; the Director has an Assistant Director under whom are project and training coordinators. The more professional wing consists of the head teachers and teachers of nursery schools under the jurisdiction of the Madrassa Resource Center. The head teachers report directly to the Director or Assistant director of the Madrassa Resource Center, usually on behalf of each nursery school's parents-teachers association committee.

The Muhaka Center is headed by a Principal, who is the Maalim (Islamic religious teacher). The principal is also directly in charge of the nursery school of the Center; the primary school is under the control of a head teacher employed by the Ministry of Education through the Teachers Service Commission (TSC). The head teacher controls his teaching staff and consults with the Center's principal on such non-educational needs of the pupils as food, and guidance and counseling. The community is represented in the activities of the Center through the parents committee. The line of authority between the head teacher and the principal on the one hand and the head teacher and the TSC on the other hand can be a source of friction.

Al-Noor Nursery and Primary School is under the direct care of the Center's Administrator. As mentioned earlier, the Administrator of the Center is answerable to an Executive Committee of the Jamia Mosque in Nairobi.

The administrative structures of the remaining three, and largely secular initiatives are relatively simple. Waa Primary School has a head teacher who is an employee of the Ministry of Education. The head teacher works cooperatively with the school committee of the parents teachers association and a special committee for the boarding section in the school. Kongowea, on the other hand as a non-formal education initiative, is under the Department of Adult Education in the Ministry of Culture and Social Services. This initiative has a head teacher who works closely with a school committee of parents. Inuka self-help Nursery and Primary School program, in contrast, is run by a Manager, who is one of the three founder doctors, a Deputy Manager, a head teacher and a deputy head teacher. The Deputy Manager handles the non-academic needs of pupils such as management of funds, food and health services while the head teacher and the deputy head teacher run the learning programs. At the time for the survey, the Inuka initiative had made no provision for the representation of parents or the community in its decision making apparatus.

8 Impact of Selected Initiatives on Wastage

In this chapter the key findings of the evaluation studies of the 20 projects are presented under the broad categories into which these projects fall. The impact of each category of projects on wastage is examined. The impact of each category of initiatives is highlighted. This is followed by an explanation of factors which have made some initiatives successful and factors which have impeded the success of others. The long term viability of some of the successful initiatives is discussed with a view to recommending those initiatives which should be expanded in the areas of their operation or replicated elsewhere in the country. Finally, gaps in research on initiatives which target the reduction of wastage in primary education are presented.

The Impact of the Different Initiatives

The assessment of impact reported here is subjective since there was no baseline studies against which one could measure gains or losses from the evaluated initiatives. In many respects, however, intended beneficiaries of the studied initiatives had no prior organized services to meet their needs.

Table 8.1 shows information on the mentioned quantitative impacts of the twenty initiatives. For a few of the initiatives, mainly those focusing on the provision of school facilities and resources, the number of persons served was overlooked. One explanation for this is that many of the initiatives which support school facilities and provide learning resources do so in existing institutions. In this sense, determining the actual number of beneficiaries would be difficult and it is permissible to assume that many of those attending the catered for institution have benefitted. In fact, a good number of this type of initiative has large spatial coverage such as one or more administrative divisions.

What can be said with certainty about the results in Table 8.1 is that the initiatives studied served a number of needy persons; in some cases the numbers served were quite large and in others numbers were rather modest. We shall show shortly that while numbers served may be a good indicator of the effectiveness of an initiative, they may not be a sufficient condition for regarding an initiative as successful. Other factors need to be taken into account.

A number of initiatives favored girls which is a good trend since girls in particular tend to suffer more hardships under poverty. Gender breakdown is not given for some of the projects, among them are Plan International and Compassion International. Many of these are also known to favor girls over boys.

The amount of resources and time invested in the studied initiatives also indicate how committed they are to improving educational opportunities to the disadvantaged groups (female and males). Our discussion with Undugu administration indicated that the center spends seventy per cent of their budget on the provision of education, training and care of children. In 1993, for example, the total budget was approximately Kshs. 80 million. The approximate figures for different activities were given as follows: Social Service Kshs. 10 million; school sponsorship Kshs. 4 million; UBEP schools Kshs. 4 million; vehicles and fuel Kshs. 50 million.

In Nadirkonyen Catholic Street Children Center, the program co-ordinator gave the following breakdown of costs: Education Kshs. 200,000; transport Kshs. 155,00; salaries Kshs. 160,000; clothes Kshs. 60,000; health 36,000; and equipment Kshs. 36,000. Wema center, on the other hand spends approximately Kshs. 150,000 per month. The director of the center indicated that monthly breakdown in terms of expenditure is as follows: Rent Kshs. 15,000; salaries Kshs. 20,000; water Kshs. 15,000; electricity Kshs. 21,000; and Kshs. 28,000 is spent on school fees every term. According to the director, the bulk of the money goes to food.

The integrated curriculum in Muslim initiatives at the coast, in addition has the advantage of reducing the education costs since the parents can now pay fees once for both types of education. In Muhaka for example each child pays an equivalent of Kshs. 25 per term in cash or kind. The Jamia Center in Turkana uses about Kshs. 50,000 per month to meet the needs of the 140 nursery children and the 40 orphans who live at the center.

Generally, the issue of budget and expenditure appeared to be very sensitive to the management of the initiatives studied. The researchers felt that several factors could explain this reluctance including: lack of proper book-keeping, lack of transparency and accountability, suspicion about competitors knowing the sources of funding, the management having no control of the budget and expenditures, among others.

The second aspect of impact considered was judgmental in nature. This involved taking into account the feelings (or better the views) of various persons associated with initiatives. The views of these individuals indicate a general impact of the initiatives on those they serve or on themselves in the case of beneficiaries. We turn next to a presentation of this aspect of impact according to the category of the initiatives.

Non-Formal Education Initiatives

The achievements of non-formal education projects visited are viewed from their main objective of providing the school age children with alternative route to basic education after missing the first chance of schooling. The pertinent issue is whether the children are rehabilitated and are going through a learning process. Are the children happy and healthy? Have they been re-routed to formal schools? Are demands for such centers increasing or decreasing?

Our study indicates that despite financial problems, all the eight centers visited were achieving their objectives in one way or the other. Destitute and street children and pregnant teenage girls had been provided with shelter, food, clothing, medical services. The biggest achievement, according to one program officer, is that these adult learners get a second chance to formal schooling: 'Seeing the children happy and healthy, and going to school is the biggest achievement that the center has attained. We are now able to provide basic education and fit them in normal local schools. The center is attracting many children from the street'. (Personal Interview: Director: Wema, 1994.)

Table 8.1 Some Quantitative Aspects of Impact of Initiatives

Type of Initiative	No. of persons served	No. of facilities	Remarks
Non-Formal Education			
Nadirkonyen Center	1991-94: 128 girls and 38 boys	1 Center	Serves very pastoralist children
Baringoi (Bendra) Center	Many	2 class streams in the evenings	Classes held in evening hours. Project replicated in two other areas as uniquely tailored to pastoralist conditions
Jamaa Home	About 69 girls annually	1 center with health facilities	Heavy dependence on donor funding
St. Johns Community	Some 50 pupils admitted yearly. Many have gone through the Center	1 Center with primary school and skills training	Heavy dependence on donor funding
Undugu	1994: 99 girls, 74 boys in one center Pumvani (Many children served)	4 basic education centers	Heavy dependence on donor funding

Table 8.1 Some Quantitative Aspects of Impact of Initiatives (cont'd)

Pandpieri Center	1980-92: 645 pupils. Many of them boys	3 sub-centers	Support of the Catholic Church essential. 956 street children said to have benefitted since 1980
Kisumu Evening Classes	1994: 110 girls, 10 boys in urban centers; 20 girls in rural sector	4 urban centers, 1 rural center	70 pupils sat for end of primary school examination and 15 passed between 1989 and 1993
Wema Center	1994: 42 girls housed	1 center for primary education	

School Facilities and Resources

Action Aid Kariobangi	About 464 pupils each year	4 primary schools	Full scholarships for poor children. Support with school building and learning resources
Christian Children's Fund (Samburu)	1983-93: 80 pupils in one center alone (many children served)	23 primary schools and 8 pre-schools in 4 divisions	Has wide coverage and encouraged enrolment of nomadic children

Table 8.1 Some Quantitative Aspects of Impact of Initiatives (cont'd)

Wamba Community Project (Samburu)	Many	Most primary schools in Wamba division	Many pastoralist students sensitized about schooling and supported materially
Plan International - Embu	Many	A number of primary schools in Siakago and Gachoka divisions	The poor relieved from costs of education
Compassion International - Embu	Many	A number of primary schools in Gachoka division	Poor children assisted to attend school
Stephan Kanja School	Many	1 regular school	Has improved performance in end of primary examination
Community Initiatives			
Madrassa Resource Center	1994:623 children in nursery schools; 693 in primary	1 training center for pre-school teachers; 14 nursery teachers	Nursery school children channeled to regular schools and hardly repeat or dropout

Table 8.1 Some Quantitative Aspects of Impact of Initiatives (cont'd)

Kongowea School	1994: about 400 pupils, most of them girls	1 center	Low cost of education and attractive to parents with children in the formal school system
Inuka Self Help School	About 400 in primary school, 60 of whom board, 40 pupils in nursery school	1 nursery school, 1 primary school	Payment of fees was later introduced leading to withdrawal by poor children
Waa Primary School	1993: 384 girls and 290 boys	1 primary school	Low cost boarding arrangements for girls. Increased female enrolment in upper grades
Muhaka Islamic School	1994: 64 pupils in nursery schools, about 100 in primary school	1 primary school and 1 nursery school	
Al-Noor Nursery School	1994: 120 children in nursery school, 40 residential office, 10 pupils supported in local primary school	1 center, 2 outpost Islamic Centers in Machakos	Since program started about 90 poor children have been rehabilitated to 2 Machakos Centers

Indeed, what the Director of Wema Center expressed applied to the seven non-formal education centers studied. The co-ordinator of Nadirkonyen Center described the achievement of the center by saying that: 'The nutrition and health of the children have greatly improved, and around 180 children have already been rehabilitated. The center follows up children who have been routed into schools and meets all their educational needs. They are taken to hospital when they are sick and in my view the center has contributed to retention and access in primary education in the district.' (Personal Interview, Coordinator: Lodwar, 1994.) The children who are re-routed to normal schools perform just as well as other children in the schools. It was reported to us that initially the head teachers of formal schools rejected children from the centers because of perceived negative influence on their pupils. But because most of those enrolled from the center(s) are doing well in their coursework such attitudes no longer exist.

A beneficiary at the same center expressed similar positive sentiments as follows: '..the center provides us with education, all needs free of charge, we are taught cleanliness, we are able to bathe everyday. Brother takes us to boarding schools and back. We are given clothes which we did not have before. We have access to electricity, playing grounds and others. If it was not for the Nadirkonyen Center we would have possibly been dead out there in the streets because of being poisoned or eating spoilt food.' (Personal Interview, Beneficiary, Nadirkonyen Center, 1994.) One of the key informants at Jamaa Center indicated that 70 per cent of the girls at the center succeed in life. The achievement of the center was described in the following words: 'We are so happy with our girls. They do so well once they get out of here. One of our ex-trainees has succeeded to become a lawyer and her experience at the center has made her so sensitive to girls in such circumstances. It is good to see such good turn outs.' (Personal Interview, Informant: Jamaa Home, 1994.) Similarly, one girl at Wema center expressed her satisfaction in Kiswahili as follows: 'Siku hizi ninapata chakula, paliali pa kulala na sishikwi na baridi kama zamani wakati nilikua sijakuja hapa. Naflirai kwa sababu sasa naweza kusoma na kuandika. Najua kushona sweta pia.' (Personal Interview, Beneficiary: Wema Center, 1994.) The English translation is: 'Now I get food to eat, a place to sleep and I don't feel cold as I used to before joining the center. I am very happy that now I can read and write. I also know how to knit a sweater.'

Although some of the centers are small and cater for few disadvantaged children in their respective districts, what they have achieved are remarkable. They have in their own way, through non-formal education, improved access and retention of disadvantaged children in primary education. Baragoi (Bendera) Center for example, has already been replicated in the district. Two similar centers have already been started at Nachola and Ngilai in the district.

Initiatives on School Resources and Facilities

The School facilities and resources initiatives surveyed realized a number of achievements. First, projects made available facilities and resources such as classrooms, workshops and offices. Pupils received quality desks and chairs as well as learning materials. The provision of these facilities has lessened the burden of the cost of education. As one informant stated: 'The provision of furniture has helped both the parents and pupils because they don't pay anything for them. The program has also supplied textbooks to a good number of pupils and has therefore promoted learning among them'.

A pupil informant at one of the schools summarized the achievement of the initiative as follows: 'We have very beautiful buildings in our school. We have been provided with stationery. The school now has enough classrooms and desks which make our learning easy. Attendance in school is quite regular because we are not sent home every now and then to bring money for books and buildings.'

The provision of school facilities and resources is perceived to have increased pupil participation and retention. For all the projects, the informants were satisfied that enrolment has increased. This is particularly significant with respect to enhanced participation of pupils from low socio-economic backgrounds. One informant aptly expressed the achievement as follows with respect to the Compassion International initiative: 'Much has been achieved in respect to pupil enrolment. Since most of the sponsored pupils are from poor families, if there was no sponsorship, all these pupils none of them could be in school because they could not afford the funds needed in the school. This has really helped the pupils to enroll and remain in the school.'

Factors that have contributed to increased enrolment have also contributed to reductions in dropout rates and repetition. Many informants indicated that the supply of school facilities and resources had increased school attendance and reduced dropout rates. The initiatives helped to reduce the cost of education which is a major contributory factor to repetition and dropout.

Another important area of achievement is improvement in academic performance. The School at Wamba town in Samburu District was said to have improved its academic performance partly due to the initiative. Likewise, Stephen Kanja Primary School performs quite well in national examinations. It is reported to be one of the few schools that take most of their pupils to national schools during the selection of form one students. The Kwale primary school inspector confirmed this in stating that: 'The improved performance of this school in the Kenya Certificate of Primary Education (KCPE) was attributed to the commitment of teachers who work in collaboration with parents; the availability of teaching and learning resources that include appropriate books and an improved learning environment. In the past, before this project was launched, the school lacked adequate classrooms; it never used to do well because some classes were held under trees, hence learners were constantly subjected to the vagaries of weather.'

What is interesting about this improved performance, is that girls performed slightly better than boys. During a group interview, standard seven boys expressed their experiences as follows: 'It is quite difficult to beat the best girls in our class. Whatever methods we employ, at the end of every term we always trail them. Consequently we have now given up in trying to undo them.'

The initiatives have also raised community awareness about the importance of education. Informants in the Christian Children Fund and World Vision reported positive attitudes to schooling among the Samburu and Turkana. The community members are quite eager to get involved in development projects. The projects in Embu and Kwale also had the effect of assisting low income communities to play an active role in education. The Stephen Kanja Project by including a nursery school block sensitized the leaders of the area to the importance of pre-school education.

Community Initiatives

The findings indicate that community initiatives have played a major role in enhancing access to pre-primary and primary school, improving performance in primary and lowering wastage. The Madrassa Resource Center for example has played a major role in increasing access and performance of the Muslim children to secular education. Muhaka Islamic initiative has enabled the Muslim children to get both Islamic and secular education concurrently. The integrated curriculum such as the ones offered in Madrassa Resource Center and Muhaka initiatives has the advantage of shortening the learning period for pupils since they do not have to attend the different schools separately. Regarding one important aspect of the achievement of the Madrassa Resource Center, the Director observed that: 'The incidence of repetition is quite low amongst Muslim children who have passed through nursery schools served by our project. We conducted a tracer study on our pupils that were attending regular primary schools. We found out that learners who had passed through our project nursery schools, performed better in class work compared to other pupils.' (Personal interview, 1994.)

The Maalim of Muhaka Center indicated just how popular the center had become. He noted that: 'Our center has attracted quite a large number of pupils from neighboring schools which offer the secular curriculum only; there are appeals from parents who live far from the center that the center be turned into a boarding school to allow their children to join it.'

Similarly, the Jamia Mosque initiative did a commendable job in assisting destitute and orphaned children to gain access to schooling. Many of the children who would still be on the streets were provided with food, shelter, clothing and basic education. The fact that the initiative was re-routing children into secular schools is commendable. Since the initiative started, 90 children were promoted and transferred to two centers established in Machakos and Isiolo by the Islamic Foundation. They are centers that cater for the education of older children who are graduates of Jamia Mosque (Al-Noor Nursery School).

Waa Primary School initiative improved girls' access to education and academic performance over a two year period. The schools' computer print out for the 1993 KCPE results over a two year period indicated that there were eight girls and only two boys among the academically best ten pupils in the school. The informants also reported that the dropout rate among girls had reduced significantly. The statistics available at the school showed that there were more boys than girls enrolled in classes one to three. From standard four to eight, the number of girls in most cases was double that for boys. The head teacher of the school (a woman) explained some reasons for the improved enrolment of girls and their good performance in these words:

'Our boarding facilities from standard four onwards have allowed us to have more counseling periods with the girls. When counseling the girls, we sensitize them about the importance of education and the value of working hard and also advise them against activities that can lead to pregnancy.' (Personal interview, Mombassa, 1995.)

In conclusion, it can be stated that some of the presented views and reports about the initiatives indicate that they were playing an important role in the promotion of access to education and retention once children enrolled. This is not to deny that some problems with enrolment and retention were present. The main point is that many of the children served would most likely be worse off without the benefit of these initiatives.

In the next section of this paper, the initiatives regarded as most successful and the criteria for this view are presented. The criteria for the success of initiatives provides part of the background against which some of them were recommended for expansion and for replication. Key reasons which render other initiatives less successful are also presented briefly. In the last section, we present gaps in research revealed by this study.

Most Successful Initiatives and Reasons for Their Success

The decision about which initiatives were the most successful and the reasons for this was made after a careful discussion and rating of all the 25 initiatives studied by members of Phase 2 of the SPRED research. The panel which included eight of the nine senior researchers, all the four research assistants and the Research and Planning Advisor, held intensive discussions for two days. What appear below are the outcomes of the panel discussions.

To start with, twenty five of the written projects were rated on some 38 criteria and accordingly ranked. Some key aspects of the 38 criteria included the following:

1. The number of beneficiaries with an emphasis on girls and those who were considered disadvantaged.

2. The extent to which the initiative had succeeded in increasing access to formal schools, non-formal education, and in providing technical/life and other skills.

3. The extent to which the initiative had succeeded in increasing retention in or reducing dropout from formal schools and non-formal education programs.

4. The extent to which the initiative had helped to improve the academic performance of the beneficiaries.

5. The extent of the reliance on donor agencies, the local community or other sources for management and administration of the initiative, the cost of personnel and salaries, consumable resources.

6. Construction and building and materials, the extent of local community involvement in accessing the provision of the initiative, their day-to-day involvement in the management and administration of the initiative, their participation in and support for the initiative.

7. The cost effectiveness of the initiative in terms of overall costs and unit cost.

8. The potential of the initiative in increasing the number of beneficiaries, expanding existing physical facilities and recruiting local staff.

9. The potential of the initiative for expansion at its present site/location, and/or at a different site/location in the same area.

10. The potential for replicability of the initiative in another part of the

country.

11. The potential for sustainability of the initiative without donor, local community or other sources of funding.

12. The extent to which expenditure levels contributed to the costs of management and administration of the initiative, the cost of personnel and salaries, consumable resources, construction and building and materials.

13. The potential for local community support for the costs of management and administration of the initiative, the cost of personnel and salaries, consumable resources, construction and building and materials.

The score for each component ranged between 5 for the most favorable rating and 1 for least favorable rating. Thus, for the 38 components rated, the highest possible score was 190 (i.e. 38 x 5 = 190) and the lowest was 38 (i.e. 38 x 1 = 38). The range on the scale was therefore between 38 and 190. None of the evaluated projects obtained the maximum score of 190 or the minimum of 38 points. The best rated project scored 146 points and the least rated had a score of 98 points, yielding a relatively smaller range of 48 points. Members of the panel proposed that all those projects scoring a total of between 146 and 126 points on the rating scale (a range of 20 points only), be regarded as the most successful initiatives. According to this decision, 14 initiatives met the criteria. Of these, 11 were among the 20 projects of concern for this paper. These 11 initiatives and the ranking each obtained were as shown in Table 8.2.

Table 8.2 Relative Ranking of Most Successful Initiatives

Theme	Project	Overall Rank	Location & District
Non-Formal Education	Baragoi out-of school Children's Center	1	Baragoi, Sarnburu
	Nadirkonyen Catholic Children Center	12	Lodwar, Turkana
Community Initiatives	Muhaka Islamic Center Madrassa Resource	2	Diani, Kwale
	Center	3	Mombassa town
	Waa Primary School (Boarding for Girls)	4	Ngombeni, Kwale
	Kongowea Community	8	Kongowea, Mombassa
School Facilities & Resources	Stephen Kanja Primary School	5	Majimboni, Kwale
	Plan International Christian Children's	7	Embu
	Fund	11	Sambru
	Action Aid, Korogocho, Primary School	13	Kariobangi, Nairobii
	Compassion International	13	Embu

What now remains is to outline those factors which make some initiatives more successful than others. The underlying principles in considering evaluated projects as successful included their contribution to improving access and retention in basic education programs (primary school and non-formal education) at affordable cost, particularly among groups considered poor or in some way disadvantaged. The factors which made the projects successful in this respect are outlined below.

The first factor which has made the initiatives to be regarded as successful was their focus on serving disadvantaged children especially girls. Most of the projects had very clear objectives related to uplifting the condition of poor children. In spite of their own financial limitations many of the initiatives were able to provide such basic needs as shelter, food, clothing, medical and counseling services for poor and destitute children.

Second, the projects allowed poor children to have access to formal or non-formal education. Sometimes children in non-formal educational programs were re-routed back to formal education where they performed quite well. Other children from non-formal schools who for one reason or another could not be admitted to formal schools, were admitted into vocational centers for skills training.

A related point regarding the success of some of the projects was their ability to increase the retention of many disadvantaged children in formal education. A good number of centers offering non-formal education followed the curriculum of formal schools. Thus, the various centers or projects made many disadvantaged children to be committed to education and skills training for the world of work.

Projects which were particularly successful in retaining disadvantaged children were those with low charges, especially for education. Most of such initiatives were charging low fees; or they had the pupils' fees paid by specific sponsors. In some cases, parents or guardians of pupils were allowed to pay in-kind, such as through contribution of materials and labor rather than in cash which many could not afford. Because of the reduced fee burden, many parents and guardians were willing to send children to these formal or non-formal schools.

The successful projects also had sound management practices which kept the costs of operating them low. Much of this sound management took the form of collaboration with a number of interested parties in promoting the goals of the projects. Sponsors of some of the projects cooperated with Government Ministries, NGOs, and other groups in the provision of their services. Some cost-sharing governed this collaboration with each party paying less than would be the case without the collaboration. For instance, in some of the educational initiatives, the MoE provided trained teachers while other partners provided desks and chairs, textbooks and other learning materials.

Related to the foregoing factor was strong commitment to work and to the goals of the initiative by some key staff. Such personnel made great sacrifices, knew what they were doing and were on the whole motivated to help disadvantaged school children. While this devotion to duty was quite pronounced within community initiatives, it was also seen in a number of other projects. At least the projects studied revealed clearly that some of the initiatives achieved their goals due to the vision and devotion to duty by their key officers.

The most successful initiatives were also able to acquire valuable resources and facilities so necessary in promoting effective learning. For instance, some projects devoted to the promotion of basic education provided classrooms, desks and chairs, textbooks, dormitories, food and clothing. Such initiatives also regularly monitored the use of these facilities and resources. The provision and maintenance of the resources and facilities through effective sponsorship opened up access to education for many disadvantaged children.

Another factor that contributed to the success of those initiatives that were able to attract ample resources, was the honest and responsible utilization of the resources by project personnel. Because of this transparency and accountability, project officers had the confidence of various sponsors and were thus able to attract more resources including funds for new programs.

Additionally, the involvement of parents and the community in the activities of the initiatives also contributed to their success. Those initiatives which involved members of the local community from the very start and which maintained a consultative working relationship with them, enhanced their record of success. Working in concert with communities encouraged them (the communities) to identify and articulate their various needs and to prioritize them. Involvement thus increased the community's awareness about the importance and relevance of various programs for their children and themselves. Projects with strong community acceptance and involvement stand a greater chance of being sustained when direct external sponsorship ends.

In certain respects the support of communities for some of the projects and the retention of pupils depended on improved academic performance. A number of initiatives therefore were considered as successful because they improved the academic performance of the learners. This was true of formal education programs especially those receiving support for facilities and resources and also non-formal education programs. For example the District Education Board (DEB) school in Wamba supported by World Vision, Stephen Kanja Primary School supported by rich tourists, reported increased attendance, retention and improved academic performance among their pupils. Similar reports came from non-formal education programs at Nadirkonyen in Lodwar town, Turkana and Jamaa Home for pregnant school girls in Nairobi.

Another factor which contributed to the success of initiatives was their integrated curriculum and activities. This was particularly the case for

Muslim children in projects evaluated in Mombassa and Kwale. Integration of Islamic education with secular education led to the retention of many Muslim children in formal and non-formal educational programs.

Some projects also succeeded because they had sound or flexible methods of recruiting and handling disadvantaged children. A number of initiatives that handled street children had staff who knew good techniques of selecting the children for their centers. Similarly, educational programs offered to the children recruited from the streets were flexible in their admission and promotion standards. For example, the level of knowledge of the learner and not chronological age was more important in assignment to a class; and children could move to the next class depending on amount of knowledge acquired and not on years completed.

Lastly, some initiatives were regarded as successful because their officers were taking steps to ensure sustainability when sponsorship ends. For example, in a few of the initiatives considered successful, community development and related agencies did mount campaigns to prepare the communities to take over the financing and management of the projects when sponsorship expires. Notable cases were Compassion International and Stephen Kanja School project.

Less Successful Initiatives and Contributing Factors

Members of the research panel for Phase 2 of the SPRED study were of the view that all those initiatives which failed to obtain a rating score of 126 points and above, were less successful. A careful examination of the written case studies by members of the SPRED research team, revealed a number of common weaknesses which made such initiatives to operate less efficiently and effectively. The common weaknesses were identified and highlighted at a joint seminar where the initiatives were also rated and ranked. Essentially, these weaknesses centered around inadequate involvement in some projects by members of local communities, insufficient resources and physical facilities, poor management of the affected initiatives, heavy dependence on donor resources and a reduced ability to retain beneficiaries such as street and slum children.

To start with, less successful projects tended to be those which were initially started without adequate consultation with the local communities. This often meant that the objectives were not clearly explained nor were the communities sufficiently sensitized before the initiatives were launched. In such cases, community members were not aware of the initiatives and were therefore not involved. Good examples were Jamia Mosque Project and Inuka Self Help School where the involvement of local communities was minimal.

Second, many of the initiatives faced the problem of inadequate physical facilities and resources. Inadequate space was a serious handicap particularly for non-formal education initiatives such as Wema, Jamaa and Pand Pieri Centers. Such community initiatives as Al-Noor (Jamai Mosque), Inuka and Kongowea Schools also had serious shortages of physical facilities and resources.

Management was also a common problem among the weaker initiatives. For instance, the Al-Noor Nursery school in the Jamia Mosque in Turkana was being barely managed by a new and inexperienced administrator. There seemed to be a conflict over the management of the Kongowea Community School between representatives of the Ministry of Education and those of the Ministry of Culture and Social Services. Such tension made for difficulties in running the school. At Jamaa Home which caters for pregnant girls, the chain of command in the management of the center was unclear. It seems as if the sister superior was the overall in charge, but she did not interact directly with the center and was probably not aware of the actual problems which existed there.

Lack of trained personnel also appeared to be a common problem with many of the weaker initiatives. Some educational initiatives did not only lack materials such as books, but they also lacked sufficient numbers of trained teachers. In the Kongowea Community School for example, the children were placed into four groups and taught at the same time by a few teachers despite their different levels of ability. At the Jamia Al-Noor Center over 60 children were taught by one teacher. In the Kisumu Evening Classes Initiative, many of the teachers in a good number of initiatives were untrained.

The initiatives targeting slum and street children experienced some peculiar problems. Some of the children who had been in the streets for long, found it hard to adjust to school schedules. Consequently some of them found it difficult to break old street habits and norms like drug abuse and smoking. Also because these children were used to handling money, which was not readily available at the centers, some of them immediately ran back into the streets whenever opportunity allowed. These kinds of problems were quite common in the urban based centers such as St. Johns Community, Action Aid Kariobangi, both in Nairobi, and Pandpieri Center in Kisumu.

Another major weakness with many of the initiatives including the ones which had been rated relatively successful, was the heavy reliance on donor support. A good number were successful on outcome factors such as the clientele they captured, increasing access, retention, improving academic performance and being cost-effective, but however tended to fair badly on issues of reliance on donor agencies for management and operational costs. They were difficult to sustain without donor funding. In this group was to be found Action Aid, Undugu Basic Education Program, and Jamaa Home all in Nairobi.

Finally, there was a lack of formative evaluation of the initiatives and programs they offered so as to establish strengths and weaknesses and future directions. The effectiveness of many of the initiatives was not formally monitored. If such evaluations existed in some of the initiatives, they were not made available to the researchers who usually inquired whether the results of such evaluations were available. There was a general feeling that such reports were confidential or that the approval of headquarter office was required.

Identification of Initiatives for Replication and/or Expansion

It will be recalled that one aspect of the Terms of Reference required the SPRED research team from the BER to 'identify those practices (innovations and experiments) which should be promoted and expanded in scale'. In effect, members of the research team felt compelled to apply even more stringent criteria to the 14 projects that had made the grade of 'most successful initiatives.' Thus, the 14 projects were re-assessed for purposes of deciding which of them should be expanded and replicated, and which should only be expanded.

The criteria for re-assessment focused on the contribution of the various projects to the increased participation of disadvantaged children in educational programs. The specific factors rated were the initiatives' contribution to the education of disadvantaged children and especially girls, their increasing access to formal and non-formal schools, increasing retention in both types of schools, increasing academic performance of the learners and the extent to which they were cost-effective.

On the basis of the new criteria, the 11 more successful initiatives of interest to this study, changed the order of priority slightly. It is instructive that all 7 of the 14 initiatives that were initially recommended as the most successful dominated that category which was recommended for both expansion and replication. Table 8.3 has these results.

Table 8.3 Recommended Action for Successful Initiatives

Projects	New rank*	Old rank
a) Projects for both expansion and replication		
Nadirkonyen Catholic Street Children's Center (Non-formal education)	1	12
Plan International (school Facilities and Resources)	2	7
Action Aid Kariobangi (School facilities and resources)	3	13
Stephen Kanja Primary School (School facilities and resources)	4	5
Baragoi Out of School Children's Center (Non-formal education)	5	1
Christian Children's Fund (School facilities and resources)	6	11
Muhaka Islamic Center (Community initiative)	7	2
b) Projects for expansion only		
Kongowea Community School (Community initiative)	8	8
Madrassa Resource Center (Community initiative)	9	3
Compassion International (School facilities and resources)	12	13
Waa Primary School (Community initiative)	13	4

* Three initiatives in the original 14 are not the focus of this study and have been omitted.

What is suggested by the results in Table 8.3 is that when it comes to considerations purely of access, retention and performance of poor children and particularly girls, the first seven initiatives were found to be the most critical. It is not surprising that the category is dominated by initiatives devoted to the provision of school facilities and resources since these are more critically related to participation in schooling (Ministry of Education, 1993 and 1994; Heyneman and Jamison, 1980; Crossley and Murphy, 1994; World Bank, 1988).

The second group of projects, those for expansion only, is dominated by community initiatives. Since community initiatives arise out of unique circumstances, replicating such initiatives elsewhere may be difficult if not actually unwise. It makes better sense for such initiatives to be expanded in their places of operation for them to have wider outreach and impact.

There were resource implications in expending and replicating the recommended initiatives. These implications needed to be coasted to finally determine which projects could reasonably be acted upon. It was not possible for the BER team to handle this task as none of the members had expertise in economics and/or financial planning and forecasting. The Terms of Reference were also silent on this particular point.

With the above observations made, we turn next to the final focus of this paper, the detected gaps in research that emerged from the experience and findings of the BER research team in Phase 2 of the SPRED operational research.

Gaps in Research

Many research issues were discernable from the findings of this operational research. The intention here is to present only a few which appeared to be prominent. We list these below.

- From the survey of initiatives targeting marginalized groups such as slum communities and pastoralists, it was apparent that they had high aspirations and interest in the education of their children. It is suggested that more research should be carried out among these communities to establish their real attitudes towards schooling instead of working from assumptions that they have negative attitudes to education.

- To attain sustainability, some initiatives had introduced the cost-sharing system with communities. While this approach seemed to work well with more economically able communities, cost-sharing may work to the detriment of the marginalized groups. More research needs to be conducted to establish viable methods of cost-sharing in such contexts.

- Although it was established that initiatives involving communities in their management were on the whole successful, the limited time for the study made it difficult to research deeply into the nature and modalities of community participation. This needs to be done in the future.

- Many of the project personnel that were interviewed in this study either did not know or were reluctant to reveal the costs of the various activities of their projects. As a result much of the little information about project costs provided in this study were either sketchy or unreliable. A study which focuses strongly on the cost of projects' activities, especially those projects which are rated highly in this report for replication and expansion, should be undertaken as a matter of urgency.

- Research is required for identifying correlates of successful initiatives and schools with good examination (academic) performance.

- Research is also required on the types of user charges in primary schools and their contribution to wastage at this level of schooling.

- Given that non-formal education programs are on the increase for children and youth in Kenya, there is a need for an intensive study to map out who are involved, and in what ways, in the provision of such programs. The end product could be a directory of providers for given districts and towns and greater attention to quality of the curricula.

- Finally, a feasibility study should be undertaken into the training needs of and training strategies for non-formal education personnel in Kenya.

9 Wastage in Developing Countries: Insights from Kenya

Nearly 130 million children in the developing world do not attend school. These children mostly belong to poor households and are the very children who need an education to pull themselves out of poverty. The consequences of non-enrolment in the world today has the potential to widen the gap between the haves and have nots. Nearly two thirds of the population non-enrolled is girls. As was discussed in Chapter three, children in rural areas, urban slums, ethnic minorities and communities in arid regions in general have very high non-enrolment rates. Particularly in South Asia as compared to the rest of the developing regions, a significantly higher proportion of girls than boys do not attend school. As a s result, a high proportion of those who will be trapped in poverty in the near future will be women. The magnitudes of gender gap in South Asian countries is unevenly distributed. The two predominantly Muslim populations in Pakistan and Bangladesh have different levels of gender gap in terms of enrollment. The gender gap is very high in Pakistan. Bangladesh reports low gender gap levels.

While the long term consequence of non-enrolment and dropout is poverty, the immediate consequence is illiteracy. The population of illiterates in the world increased from 860 million in 1970 to 895 million in 1990. Even though there has been some decline in the number of illiterates world wide in the nineties, the number is likely to still remain high, at about 830 million by the end of this decade.

The prevalence of non-enrolment and dropout is higher in the African countries than in the rest of the developing regions. In about 18 Sub-Saharan African countries, more than fifty percent of the population 25 years and older never had primary level schooling. Even in Africa, the distribution is uneven as is noted in Chapter 1. Low levels of enrolment in the Sahel countries coexist with high enrolment levels of nearly 90 percent, in countries like Zimbabwe and Botswana. Slightly more than 50 percent of Africa's primary school-age children are not in school and less than half of those entering first grade will complete their primary education. Many will dropout before they acquire minimal levels of literacy and numeracy.

In general then, on one side of the coin, the developing world today is saddled with levels of non- enrollment and dropout that are unacceptable by the standards that have been pronounced at world conferences such as the one held in Jomtien, Thailand, in 1990. As as result, the divide between haves and have-nots is likely to increase with more young women than men, and special groups such as ethnic minorities bearing the brunt of the cruel consequences of illiteracy.

On the other side of the coin, there are several noticeable positive aspects. In the past fifty years, the total number of children enrolled in primary school world wide has increased more than three hundred percent. Even in Africa, where non- enrollment is high, primary school enrolment increased more than ten times since 1950. Developing countries as a whole have achieved a net primary school enrolment ratio above eighty percent. Net enrolment ratios are especially high in East Asia, Latin America, and the Caribbean, where enrolment ratios are above 95 percent. In both developed and developing countries excluding Sub-Saharan Africa and the Arab States, the number of primary school-age children who are not enrolled in school steadily declined from 127 million in 1990 to approximately 113 million in 1998. Among these out of school children, 110 million live in the developing countries.

As mentioned in Chapter 5, enrolment ratio in Kenya is in general high with members of a few special groups and young girls being disproportionately represented in the non-enrolled and school dropout population. During the last three decades there was a remarkable expansion in the number of children enrolled in primary schools. Even more impressive is the noticeable increase in the proportion of girls in the primary school going population. At independence, only about a third of enrolment in primary schools were girls. By 1990 the proportion of girls had risen to nearly 50 per cent. In the following paragraphs we attempt to relate findings from our study to broad program and policy goals.

The most important cause of non-enrolment was parental ignorance including neglect of girls education. Wage employment of children was also identified as another significant cause of non-enrolment. Teachers often view parents as being uneducated and uninterested. The outcome of such wide spread feelings is that the community, for its part, feels little sense of responsibility towards the school. The community seldom finds interests, values and concerns addressed in the school curriculum. The lack of dialogue between school and the community interferes with the ability of the school to influence family and community based factors which result in dropout. Lloyd, Mensch, and Clark (1998) suggest that the likelihood of dropout among girls is influenced by family factors. For boys, school factors appear to be more important. The lack of communication between the community and school considerably reduces the ability of school to prevent the high rates of dropout among girls.

In Kenya, the presence of PTAs in most schools is a resource of immense value. The effective use of PTAs to implement changes may be constrained by the presence of excessively centralized administration and poor management at all levels. In many instances those who administer are individuals with little training in administration or management. Most decisions are taken by central administrators with very little involvement in the day to day working of the schools. As a result, many of these administrative decisions fail to take into account the realities experienced in classrooms and communities.

One of the causes of grade repetition was identified as inadequate school resources. This is a wide spread problem not only in Kenya but also among educational systems in other sub Saharan countries. A very high proportion of the available resources is spent in teacher salaries. About 90 percent of the available resources in school systems in Sub Saharan Africa is spent on teacher salaries. The lack of availability of desks, chairs, text books and adequate buildings contribute to poor school climate resulting in apathy among teachers, and the motivation among teachers is often low. Teachers feel neglected by the community in general. Under such conditions, the lack of trust between community and school is likely to be strained. The rigid administrative style also contributes to the lack of flexibility in using resources left over from paying teacher salaries.

A second cause of grade repetition was due to selected children being held back from appearing for the Kenya Primary School Examination. The objective of forced grade repetition is to improve school performance at the primary school examinations. The factors which cause this grade repetition may very well be school related. Poor pedagogy and poor teacher training may be associated with this. In many Kenyan schools, the teachers usually have only a modest level of education themselves and have undergone little systematic training. Teachers often tend to overemphasize rote learning rather than using active methods. Very few teachers have experience in organizing programs that can cater to students of different achievement levels. Very few countries have effective programs of continuing education for teachers to help them learn new ways of teaching. Often, the teachers do not posses instructional guides to guide them on how to present subjects and organize related classroom activities.

The fact that many parents cannot afford to send their children to school because of large school levies raises issues about national commitment to education. Enabling parents to send their children to school then may not be approached merely as a education institutional problem, but as a problem of economic and social development. From this point of view, the current global attention on reproductive health, primary school education and sustainable environment may be exploited to formulate integrated programs of health and development founded on the basis of universally accessible primary school education. It is important to associate approaches to education to wider development programs involving policies on sanitation, transport and health. For example, distance to school was mentioned as one of the reasons for low enrollment and dropout. Yet, the school system is often unable to respond to it well lacking educational sectoral linkages with transportation sector.

If education is seen as a valuable commodity, lack of access to this valuable commodity may be seen as a human rights issue. From a national security and development point, the presence of even one child unable to access a primary education may be seen as one too many. If a country is to develop all children without exception then, all children have to have at least the basic skills of literacy and arithmetical skills. Education enables individual to acquire more income, improve their health and nutrition intake. In addition, literates are more capable of utilization of knowledge and information than illiterates.

From a human rights perspective, the inability to pay for primary schooling should no longer prevent eligible children from attending primary schools. Our study found that some of the more successful initiatives for preventing wastage were the ones with either low school fees or where parents were allowed to pay in kind when unable to make cash payments. The benefits of education are even more significant for girls. Research studies show that women with as little as four years of education are more likely to have smaller, healthier families (Lloyd, Mensch and Clark, 1998).

Provision of boarding schools mainly for girls was offered as a solution to encourage girls enrollment by head teachers. This was also part of the solution proposed by head teachers to prevent repetition. Underlying these proposed solutions is the awareness that girls often are engaged in domestic chores and are therefore more constrained than boys in finding time to devote to studies. This concern was also expressed by head teachers in their proposal to reduce the level of domestic chores at home to prevent dropout among girls. Girls are also affected by gender based stereotyping. Lloyd, Mensch and Clark (1998) found that variables measuring gender differences in treatment were significant for girls. Furthermore, school which discriminate in favor of boys were found to have higher dropout rates in Kenya.

Policies and programs must be initiated to remove curriculum contents, books and classroom activities that directly or indirectly provide sexual stereotypes at all levels of primary education. Teachers and all educational personnel must be trained in treating boys and girls equally. The training courses should focus on enabling teachers to maintain gender neutrality in the conduct of the class as well in the use of vocabulary.

Even as Kenyan school remain accessible to these children, the needs of these young girls are unique, and the support structure they need to keep themselves in school may be different from those demanded by boys and girls who have not dropped out. In developing countries these issues are being addressed by the opening of second chance educational programs. These schools provide training in a trade or craft to enable them earn a living own their own. These centers are staffed by women groups and engage local craftsmen to teach arts and crafts to girls.

Given the positive contributions of girls education to the long term improvement of the economy and national well being, it is necessary to investigate the determinants of family based disadvantages young girls suffer in terms of high non- enrollment, repetition and dropout rates than boys. The vulnerabilities of specific groups such as girls point to the persisting influence of social inequality within the institutions of family. Even as much as these inequalities constrain educational opportunities for girls, they also influence other aspects of personal well being such as health.

To focus on primary school education among girls without paying attention to health could be self defeating. School could play an important role here. The problem of teenage pregnancy, and sexual exploitation of girls should be addressed through the introduction of reproductive health education in schools. Thus improvement in primary school education among girls is a reliable indicator of true gains in the removal of structural inequalities within the family setting. In our study, all successful initiatives, community and school based, were successful in reducing repetition and dropout among girls.

We propose the set up of a national committee composed of senior government officials responsible for education, and senior representatives of organizations promoting women's welfare. The committee should examine the existing imbalances in educational opportunities between boys and girls; and also investigate the factors that contribute to non-enrolment, repetition and dropout among girls.

Mobilization and sensitization of community to parents was the most preferred solution to increase enrollment, reduce repetition and dropouts. Effective public relations strategies through the use of media must be developed to raise the awareness of parents with regard to education in selected areas. Multi-pronged communication strategies including the use of spot announcements, theater, and songs to convey appropriate messages should be developed. Mobilization of the community for education will not occur without the participation of local communities in identifying the objectives of the school. As indicated a earlier, a near universal presence of PTAs in Kenyan schools is an invaluable resource in eliciting the participation of the community. In this regard all mobilization programs should reach out to the community initially. The negative attitudes that teachers may have about parents should be removed to begin successful school community relationship. Teachers and local educational personnel should receive training in community organization and development. What is needed is a cadre of educational personnel, strongly committed to work and goals of primary schools through collaboration with the community. This study found a strong association between success of an initiative and work commitment. Given the emphasis we have placed on girls education, the presence of adequate representation of women in PTAs is essential for addressing and developing programs targeted towards improving primary school education among girls.

A useful entry point for the school into the community is in the area of eradication of adult illiteracy. Adult literacy programs are valuable not only in removing illiteracy in the community, but also in promoting the value of primary education for girls and boys. In the long haul, the effectiveness of the school community collaboration will to an extent depend upon the amount of readiness among educational personnel to accommodate the values and needs of the community. One specific way of demonstrating the willingness among educational personnel to accommodate the values of the community is by attempting to make school schedules flexible. In our study we found that initiatives which developed integrated curriculums responding to the needs of the community were much more successful in reducing wastage than initiatives which were not responsive to the community. In addition, these initiatives maintained a high level of accountability and made responsible use of resources.

At the international level, the amount of money available from donor agencies to support primary school education developing countries has decreased over time. Aid from the World Bank has dropped from 1,487 to 880 million. Most European countries have promised an outlay of 0.7 percent of their gross national product for supporting education in developing countries. In the recent times most of these donor countries except, Nordic states, have failed to donate the promised amounts. The reduction in donor support for education in developing countries may result in collapse of current donor supported initiatives. Coordination and efficient management of donor supported activities is essential for utilization of available support for reducing, non- enrollment, repetition and dropout in the developing countries. In addition, it is necessary to begin to seek the support and involvement of private sector and non-governmental organizations in the area of basic education. Our study found that successful initiatives to reduce wastage had sound management and also engaged in multilateral collaboration approaches.

References

Abagi, J.O. (1993), 'Education For All in Kenya: Improving Access and Retention of Marginal Groups within the School System', *Basic Education Forum*, vol.3.

Achola, P.P.W.(1989), *Educational Opportunities for Vulnerable Groups in Kenya*, prepared on behalf of Bureau of Educational Research, Nairobi: Kenyatta University.

Achola, P.P.W.and Shiundu, J.O. (1991a), 'Education and Literacy', in *A Household Welfare Monitoring and Evaluation Survey of South Nyanza District*, Nairobi: Ministry of Planning and National Development.

Achola, P.P.W., and Shiundu, J.O. (1991b), 'Basic Education and Literacy', in *A Household Monitoring and Education Survey of Baringo District*, Nairobi: Ministry of Planning and National Development/UNICEF.

Achola, P.P.W., and Shiundu, J.O. (1991c), 'Basic Education and Literacy', in *A Household Monitoring and Education Survey of South Nyanza District*, Nairobi: Ministry of Planning and National Development/UNICEF.

Achola, P.P.W., Shiundu, J.O. and Orodho, J.A. (1991), 'School Wastage in Kenya with Special Reference to ASALS: A State-of-the-Art Review', Kenyatta University: Bureau of Educational Research.

Achola, P.P.W., Shiundu, J.O. and Orodho, J.A. (1992), 'School wastage in Kenya with special reference to ASALS: A state-of-the-Art review', Kenyatta University, Bureau of Educational Research: Child Survival and Development Project.

Ahai, D. (1988), Towards a National System of Education in Kenya, in T. O. Eisemon, *Benefitting from Basic Education, School Quality and Functional Literacy in Kenya*, Oxford and New York: Pergamon Press, pp. 130-142.

Bowles, S. and Aintis, H. (1976), *Schooling in Capitalist America: Educational Reform and the Contradictions of Economic Life*. New York: Basic Books.

Briggs, H. (1973), *A Study of the Premature Withdrawal of Students from Primary Schools in Kenya*, M.A. (Ed.) Thesis, University of Nairobi.

Chaptegei, I.C. (1982), *Enrolment Trends for Primary Schools 1970-1978, (P.G.D.E. Project)*, Kenyatta University. Nairobi.

Chege, A. (1983), *Education for Masaai Girls, Socio-Economic Background*, M.A. (Ed.) thesis, University of Nairobi.

Combs, J. and Cooley, W. (1968), 'Dropouts: In High School and After High School', *American Educational Research Journal*, vol.5(3), pp.343-363.

Crossley, M. and Myra Murby (1994), 'Textbook Provision and the Quality of School Curriculum in Developing Countries: Issues and Policy Options', *Comparative Education*, vol. 30(2), pp.99-114.

Dutta, A. (1984), *Education and Society: A Sociology of African Education*, New York: St. Martins Press.

Ekstrom, R. B., Avertz, M. E., Pollack, J. M. and Rock, D. A. (1986), 'Who Drops Out of High School and Why?', *Teachers College Record*, vol.87,(3), pp. 356-373.

Eshiwani, A.S. (1984), *A Study of Women's Access to Higher Education in Kenya with Special Reference to Mathematics and Science*, Kenyatta University: Bureau of Educational Research (mimeo).

Eshiwani, A.S., Achola, P.P.W. and Sena, S.O. (1988), *Education in a Semi-Arid Area: A Study of Determinants of School Achievement in Kajiado District*, Kenyatta University: Bureau of Educational Research.

Finn, J. D. (1989), 'Withdrawing from School', *Review of Educational Research*, vol.59(2), pp.122-133.

Gichia, K. (1992), 'Automatic Promotion in Primary Schools in Kenya: Its Implications in Curricula and Other Related Areas', *Basic Education Forum*, vol.2.

Gitau,W. (1985), *A Study of Factors Related to Early School Withdrawal in Primary Schools in Kiambu District*, M.Ed. Project, Nairobi: Kenyatta University.

Government of Kenya (1989), *Kenya Country Paper for Eastern and Southern Africa Regional Consultation on Education For All*. Nairobi: Government Press.

Government of Kenya (1992), *Education for All (EFA): Issues and Strategies, 1991-2000 and Beyond*. Nairobi: Government Press.

Government of Kenya Ministry of Education. (1997), *Education Sector Analysis*, No.8, Nairobi: Ministry of Education.

Grissom, J. B. and Shepard, L. A. (1989), 'Repeating and Dropping Out of School', in Shepard, L. A. and Smith, M. L. (eds.), *Flunking Grades: Research and Policies on Retention*. London: Falmer Press, pp.302-316.

Harvey, G and Klein, S.S. (1989), *Equity in Education*, New York: Palmer Press.

Harvey, G. and Noble, G. (1985), 'The Preferred Shape of the Distribution Curve or Just Distribution of Economic Resources in Society', in *Handbook of Achieving Sex Equity Through Education*, Baltimore & London: The John Hopkins Press.

Heyneman, S.P. and Jamison, D. (1980), 'Textbook Availability and Other Determinants of Student Learning in Uganda', *Comparative Education Review*, vol. 24, pp. 206-220.

Heyneman, S.P. and Loxley, W. (1983), 'Influences on Academic Achievement across 29 High and Low Income Countries', *American Journal of Sociology*, vol.88, pp. 1162-1194.

Kathuri, N.J. (1986), 'Factors that Influence the Performance of Pupils', in C. P. E. *Kenya Educational Research Awards Research Report,* No. 110, Kenyatta University: Bureau of Educational Research.

Kelly, D.M. (1995), 'School Dropouts', in Martin Carnoy (ed.) *International Encyclopedia of Economics of Education*, Second Edition, New York: Elsevier Science Ltd., pp. 308-313.

King, K. (1974), 'Primary Schools in Kenya: Some Critical Constraints on Their Effectiveness' in D. Court and D. Ahai (eds.) *Education, Society and Development: New Perspectives from Kenya*. Nairobi: Oxford University Press.

Kirui, P.M.K. (1982), *A Study of Factors that Influence the Increasing Repetition and Dropout Rates in Primary Schools in Nandi District of Kenya*, Post-graduate Diploma in Education Project, University of Nairobi.

Levy, M.B. (1971), 'Determinants of Primary School Dropout in Developing Countries', *Comparative Education Review*, vol. 15, pp. 44-58.

Lloyd, C., Mensch, B. and Clark, W. (1998). 'The Effects of Primary School Quality on the Educational Participation and Attainment of Kenyan Girls and Boys', Paper presented at the Annual meeting of the Population Association of America, 2-4 April, Chicago.

Loxley, W. (1987), 'Wastage in Education', in George Psacharopoulos (ed.) *Economics of Education: Research and Studies*, Oxford, England: Pergamon Press, pp.62-65.

Mann, D. (1986), 'Can We Help Dropouts: Thinking About the Undoable', *Teachers College Record*, vol.87(3), pp.307-323.

Masariru, K.A. (1981), *Population Trends and the Provision of Primary Education in Nairobi: Implications for Educational Planning*, M. A. thesis in Population Studies, University of Nairobi.

Meme, N.N. (1987), *An Investigation into Factors Contributing to Drop-out Problem of Girls in Primary Schools in Ithima Location of Meru District*, Post Graduate Diploma in Education Project, Nairobi: Kenyatta University.

Menya, H.O. (1992), *The National Conference on Education for All (EFA), Kenya*, Draft Report, Nairobi: Kenya National Commission for UNESCO.

Michieka, E.N. (1983), *An Investigation of the Causes of Pupils Drop-out in Primary Schools in Kisii District in Kenya*, Post-graduate Diploma in Curriculum Development, University of Nairobi.

Ministry of Education (1994), *Perceptions and Opinions of the Ministry of Education Staff Regarding Factors Associated with Wastage in Primary Education in Kenya*, Final SPRED Research Report: Nairobi, July.

Ministry of Education (1995), 'Final Report of Synthesis of Case Study Findings', SPRED Operational Research Phase 2: Nairobi.

Murphy, P. and Gipps, C. (1996), *Equity in the Classroom*, London & Washington: Palmer Press.

Mwangi, J. (1988), *Pressure for Entry into City Council Schools at the Onset of Education: A Demographic Interpretation*, Postgraduate Diploma in Population Studies, University of Nairobi.

Natricello, G. et al. (1986), 'Taking Stock: Renewing Our Research Agenda on the Causes and Consequences of Dropping Out', *Teachers College Record*, vol. 87(3), pp. 431-432.

Nderitu, C.N. (1987), *A Study of Causes of Drop-out in Primary Schools in Gichugu Division, Kirinyaga District*, M.Ed. Project, Kenyatta University.

Ngau, M.M. (1991a), *The Effects of Grade Retention and Drop-outs on the School System and Pupils*, Kenya, Uganda and Tanzania Educational Research Awards (KUTERA), International Development Research Centre (IDRC) Research Report.

Ngau, M.M. (1991b), *Grade Retention and School Drop-outs in Kenyan Primary Schools: A Critical Analysis and Equity Issues in Education*, University of California, Los Angeles, Ph.D. Dissertation.

Nguru, A. (1980). *Research on Drop-outs in Kenya*, Kenyatta University, Bureau of Educational Research (mimeo).

Nkimyangi, A. (1980), *Socio-Economic Determinants of Repetition and Early Withdrawal at Primary School Level and Their Implication for Educational Planning in Kenya*, Kenyatta University: Bureau of Educational Research (mimeo).

Nungen, M. (1997), *Affirmative Action and the Quest for Equality in Kenya*, Kenyatta University, M.Ed. Thesis.

Okumu, O. (1992), *A Study of the Female Child: The Case Study of Nairobi*, A Report compiled for ANPPCAN/CW Project, Nairobi.

Onyango, H.E.O. (1986), *Enrollment Trends in Primary Schools in Nyanza Province Since 1971*, Kenyatta University, Post Graduate Diploma in Education Project.

Porsi, F.T. (1988), *Sex and Birth Order Selective Under enrollment in Primary Schools of Kenya's semi-arid Districts and the 'Kepyions' Phenomenon*, IDS Working Paper No.462, University of Nairobi.

Raju, B.M. (1973), *Education in Kenya: Problems and Perspectives in Educational Planning and Administration*, London: Kumarian Press.

Rumberger, R. (1983), 'Dropping Out of High School: The Influences of Race, Sex, and Family Background', *American Educational Research Journal*, vol.20(2), pp.199-220.

Shiundu, J.O. and Achola, P.P.W. (1994), *Access, Participation and Performance by Slum Children in Formal Basic Education: A Study of Nairobi, Mombosa and Kisumu*, Research Report to UNICEF Kenya Country Office, Nairobi.

Sifuna, D.N. (1988), 'Kenya', in A. T. Kunan (ed.), *World Education Encyclopedia*, pp.736-759, vol.2.

Sifuna, D.N. (1989), 'The Quality of Schools and Pupils Achievement in Kenya', *Kenya Journal of Education*, vol.4(2), pp. 212-220.

Sifuna, D.N. (1992), 'Pre-vocational Subjects in Primary Schools in the 8-4-4 Education System in Kenya', *International Journal of Educational Development*, vol. 12(2).

SPRED (1994), *Perceptions and Opinions of Selected Staff of the Ministry of Education about Factors Associated with Wastage in Primary Education in Kenya*, Phase 1 Part 2, Nairobi: Ministry of Education, July.

Steinberg, L., Blinele, P. L. and Chan, K. S. (1984), 'Dropping out among language minority youth', *Review of Education Research*, vol.54, pp. 113-132.

Thias, H.H. and Carnoy, M. (1972), *Cost-Benefit Analysis in Education: A Case Study of Kenya*, Baltimore: The John Hopkins Press.

UNICEF/Government of Kenya (1992), *Children And Women In Kenya: A Situational Analysis*. Nairobi.

Wamahiu, S.P. (1992), 'The Situation of the Female Child in Kenya', Reports submitted to the Kenya Alliance for the Advocacy of Children's Rights, through the African Network for the Prevention and Protection Against Child Abuse and Neglect (ANPPCAN), Kenya Chapter, Nairobi.

World Bank (1986), *Educational Strategies for Sub-Saharan Africa*, Washington D.C.: The World Bank.

World Bank (1988), *Education in Sub-Saharan Africa: Policies for Adjustment, Revitalization and Expansion*, Washington D.C.: The World Bank.

Index